Deep Wisdom
From Shakespeare's Dramas

Deep Wisdom
From Shakespeare's Dramas

Theological Reflections on Seven Shakespeare Plays

Arjan Plaisier

Translated by Steve J. Van der Weele

Steve J. Van Der Weele

May 17, 2013

WIPF & STOCK · Eugene, Oregon

Deep Wisdom From Shakespeare's Dramas
Theological Reflections on Seven Shakespeare Plays

Wipf & Stock
An Imprint of Wipf and Stock Publishers
199 W. 8th Ave., Suite 3
Eugene, OR 97401
www.wipfandstock.com

ISBN 13: 978-1-62032-060-0
Manufactured in the U.S.A.

Translated from *Is Shakespeare ook onder de Profeten?: Theologische meditaties bij zeven stukken van Shakespeare* by Dr. Arjan Plaisier (Zoetermeer, NL: Uitgeverij Boekencentrum, 2008).

Contents

Foreword

OVER THE YEARS OF my lifetime I have been an enthusiastic reader of the works of William Shakespeare. Reading naturally and seamlessly led to writing, and this book is the outcome. I have chosen seven of Shakespeare's dramatic works for a specific approach and interpretation. I intend this admittedly limited group of seven varied and better-known works as representative of his work as a whole This variety consists of comedies, history plays, problem plays, tragedies, and tragic-comedies. Tragedies are rightly judged to be the highest of his achievements. I have devoted three of my seven essays to them.

My choice of plays for discussion is based on my own predilection but is also suitable for the interpretation I am determined to give them. In my introductory chapter I will present, in summary form, the specific interpretation I intend to provide.

The original title *Is Shakespeare also to be numbered among the Prophets?* raises questions that need answers. Just as there is a sharp distinction between an apostle and a man of genius, so is there a distance between an author and a prophet. Still, at times the distance narrows between such categories. Saul was never a prophet. Yet, after Samuel anointed him as king, people asked, on that very day, "Is Saul also to be numbered among the prophets?" We must accept Shakespeare for what he is: a playwright of world renown. But at times we cannot resist the temptation to see him wearing the mantle of a prophet—though now and then we are made to wonder whether he was serious or only playing a role.

As a theologian, I am a dilettante in the world of literature. I make no pretense to scholarly credentials. Still, sometimes the dilettante can ferret out matters that conventional scholarly research leaves undiscovered. This is the function, as an amateur, I hope to achieve. This book is intended primarily for *aficionados* and serious readers of Shakespeare. Who knows? It may also stimulate others to read Shakespeare. Great literature, to be sure, requires (and deserves) great effort, but that effort always brings about its own reward. Besides that group of readers, I write also for those who interest themselves in the subject of the influence of the Christian faith in the domain of letters. More generally still, this book is intended for those who concern themselves with the role (and works) of the imagination, a gift which can enrich the life of the Christian. Powerful works of the imagination, nourished by a Christian outlook, are not exactly in great supply nowadays. Because with effort we can throw a bridge between our age and ages gone by, we as heirs have the opportunity to enrich contemporary culture with provocative readings.

Translator's Preface

EVEN WITH MY DUTCH language acquisition somewhat dormant, I knew immediately that I was holding a book of unusual importance when I first encountered (through a colleague of the author) Dr. Plaisier's book of essays on Shakespeare. A leading Dutch pastor and lifelong student of the poet, Plaisier is chagrined at the modernization and secularization of the bard's works on the stage and in scholarly discourse. His book reminds us all that Shakespeare lived in a place and time when the Christian faith still robustly shaped the mind and art of Christian Europe. For a spectator of a production or a reader of the plays to ignore these religious underpinnings is to trivialize Shakespeare's achievement, compromise our appropriation of his thought, and squander opportunities to savor the wisdom which the plays so aptly express.

But the book goes about that task quietly. It is not polemical. Plaisier simply reports, with skill and art, what he finds in the text. His profession as a theologian equips him admirably to "mine the ore" of dramatic moments in the plays—often detecting what others have missed. He demonstrates how theology actively shapes the narrative and direction of the plays. He delineates motives, analyzes temptations, defines the nature of kingship, describes the tension between divine law and human law, and explains the archetypal force of certain characters and motifs. Plaisier's theological acumen embraces other disciplines as well—including psychology and law. He looks always for such nuances as enrich the meaning of the play.

Plaisier provides three essays besides the seven on the plays. His introduction helpfully sketches the religious and cultural setting of Shakespeare's life and times. Appendix I is addressed especially to pastors, urging them to take literature seriously as they perform their ministerial functions. He skillfully sets forth the specific resources of theology and literature separately, then shows how their intersection can enrich both landscapes. Shakespeare, he advises his colleagues, is a good place to begin. And it is true, as one reader observed, that Plaisier's essays, because of their thoroughness, make the plays accessible to people who may not be wholly familiar with the plays. Appendix II consists of a biographical sketch of Shakespeare. I have not included that chapter, assuming that such information is readily available elsewhere.

The work has been a challenge. Plaisier's "mining" goes deep. What encouraged me to undertake the task, in addition to my residual knowledge of the Dutch language, is my familiarity with these very plays, having taught them regularly during my teaching career. The effort has had its own reward for me. And I have confidence that the essays will enhance anyone's engagement with Shakespeare as Dr. Plaisier reminds us of the religious roots which shaped the mind and art of a dramatist without peer.

I record with appreciation the help of colleagues who monitored my translation efforts: Martin Bakker, Andrew Kuyvenhoven, Howard Slenk, and Sierd Woudstra. I hope Mr. Slenk will soon forget the many times I interrupted his work with a request for help on various knotty passages, of which there were not a few. My brother Ray Van der Weele and Jennie Hoekstra lent invaluable technical support.

Dr. Steve J. Van der Weele
Calvin College (Emeritus)

Shakespeare and the Christian Faith

WILLIAM SHAKESPEARE REMAINS AN enigma. How is it possible that a man out of Stratford-on-Avon, who never attended a university, who did not belong to the nobility, and who did not enjoy court support, became the author of thirty-eight dramatic works that, together, rank with the best of the world's literature? Is Shakespeare the actual author of this body of work? The question rose already in his own time and is being posed again. I will let the final answer to this question to the history specialists, and so long as no watertight evidence is proved to the contrary, I will settle for the "true" William Shakespeare.[1]

His claim to fame is incontestable. It is also true, however, that he was not for everyone in his own age. Some found him an arrogant coxcomb, unworthy of attention.[2] Nevertheless, his reputation surged already in his lifetime. After his death in 1616, solicitations went out for copies of his work. This invitation resulted in the so-called Folio edition of 1623, for which his contemporary Ben Jonson (1537–1637) wrote a moving foreword. After that, a bevy of "Testimonies to the Genius and Merits of Shakespeare"[3] made their appearance. He has long been ranked with the truly great—Homer, Dante, Cervantes, Goethe, Tolstoy, and Dostoevsky.

Shakespeare is a representative of the so-called Elizabethan Drama. Thus, he lived in a milieu when drama was at its height. Besides Shakespeare, one thinks of the work of Kyd, Marlowe, Webster, Middleton, Chapman, and Jonson. To be sure, a tradition of drama existed before Elizabethan drama—especially the miracle and mystery plays of the Middle Ages (which were still being performed in Shakespeare's day).

1. It is seldom convincing to explain one miracle by a still greater wonder and that would be the case when, contrary to a nearly unanimous voice of tradition, there appears to be a secret author.

2. The most famous example is Robert Greene, a gifted writer of dramas, who called Shakespeare "an upstart crow."

3. This is the title of the first critical anthology of texts about Shakespeare, which appeared in 1769 and was compiled by David Garrick.

One is tempted to say that the outburst of dramatic talent cannot readily be explained. Clearly, the time was ripe for this development; besides, one discerns a process of mutual influence and stimulus among these dramatists.

The Elizabethan Drama materialized at the cutting edge of two worlds. On the one hand we confront the world dominated by the Christian worldview. To be sure, the unity of the church after the Middle Ages had been shattered. Still, what cannot be denied is that the Christian faith also remained very evident in the public domain. On the other hand, the Elizabethan era is the first in modern times that witnessed the process of secularization that contributed to a significant marginalization of the Christian faith. The world in which Shakespeare grew up was in many respects larger, more complex, and intricate than the previous eras. Both movements, the Christian and the secular, contributed to the phenomenon of Shakespeare. An age without some coherent horizon of understanding, such as ours, will not very readily produce great drama. True, the Christian worldview was being challenged and even contested by new questions that provide even greater depth to these dramas. These dramas reflect the convergence of both worlds in a most intriguing way. The Christian faith in these works, it must be said, manifests itself, for the most part, not explicitly but as presuppositions. The stage in the somewhat closed world of the Middle Ages had to be hospitable to all sorts of characters who had to find their way in a world that was both attractive but also complex and risky.

It would be redundant to try to account in a comprehensive way for the genius and merit of Shakespeare. What attracts him most avidly is narrating the stories circulating in his day—stories that serve as the sources of his plays.[4] What a keen mind, to recognize the human situation in these stories, and what skill and art was his to forge these source materials into a play of five acts—the customary length of plays. What a discerning eye for the whole spectrum of human experience—from joy, marriage, friendship, feasts, rest and peace, to sorrow for the dead, murder, alienation, deception, and adultery. What an amazing sensitivity to religious

4. Shakespeare chose and studied his sources with great care. Though he was not a learned man, but a writer for the stage, we should be dumbfounded at the notion (proposed in the historically inaccurate film *Shakespeare in Love*) that Shakespeare needed no sources, that he was impulsively driven by his surging genius to write his dramas. Such an idea should be relegated to the world of fables.

attitudes, to superficiality and profundity, to wisdom and folly, to sublimity and malice, to piety, and godlessness—all perceived in their diversity and varying temperaments—and all brought to light and expressed in a way possible by only a truly great poet. What categories of people and unforgettable types. What close attention he gave to the various callings of people and the varied dispositions of the population—from the king to the beggar, from the noble to the harlot, from the army commander to the grave digger. And what is an even greater achievement: the close attention he pays to the relationship of morality and religion and the deeds of humanity—their motives, their thoughts, their deliberations—and the insights into the consequences which follow.

All in all, the works of Shakespeare constitute a study of humanity in almost unequaled depth and breadth. And all this study of humanity by someone who, with increasing power over language, like a magician plying his arts, rose to a poetic genius who produced an almost unequaled profusion of dramatic materials.

Shakespeare and Christian Belief

"Shakespeare and Christian belief" is a coupling of words that will sound strange to the ears of many. "Do not the works of Shakespeare," asks a reader rooted in a secular society, "resemble a seamless, a closed world?" And, indeed, given the way plays are produced on the stage nowadays, one will probably not discern the light of the Christian faith that pervades them. Audiences will regard references from the Bible pertaining to the Christian faith as fortuitous, without any particular overtones, and as having nothing in particular to do with the contents or the meaning of the play. This mentality is also reflected in mainstream exegesis of Shakespeare's works. A typical spokesman for this view is the poet John Masefield, who writes, "He [Shakespeare] held to no religion, save that of humanity and his own great nature." It appears as a settled matter that Shakespeare's world is that of modern secularism and that Christian insights have little or nothing to do with his plays.

This assumption, however, rests on wobbly feet. To begin with, such critics perform a curious feat: they detach Shakespeare from his own era. Whatever needs to be said about his originality, Shakespeare belongs to the culture—even subculture of the late sixteenth and early seventeenth century in England. A realistic appraisal of this awareness obliges us to say that he shared in many ways the common sense of his age. It is a tempting, but a doubtful, undertaking to account for his genius in such a way that we isolate him from this resource of *common sense*. Obviously, every age is free to impart to drama from an earlier era a new life in such a way that the result shows a parting of the way from the background materials and no longer has any affinity with them. But suppose that these elements are fundamental for the play. Then the question arises whether such an interpretation does not weaken the play. But this is just what is happening in many productions nowadays. Notwithstanding the professionalism of directors and actors, they often lose sight of the significance, the true meaning of the play. It seems as if the plays need to be made interesting for a postmodern public. Meanwhile, fundamental facets of the play are ignored or, as is frequently done, actually ridiculed.

Should we at some time again acquire the vision of the spiritual dimension of the plays which belong "naturally" to the Christian frame of reference, even if in the age of Shakespeare this frame of reference is in transition and is being contested, we will have restored the true meaning of the play, which at the present day is all too often ignored at the Bühne.

No one will be surprised to learn that studies of Shakespeare and the Christian faith have been undertaken prior to now. Here we must surely acknowledge the work of G. Wilson Knight.[5] In addition, we think of the anthology of Roy Battenhouse, *Shakespeare's Christian Dimension: An Anthology of Commentary*.[6] Peter Milward has done even more recent work in this area.[7] In many new studies—articles and other inquiries—attention is being given once again in a more general way to the relationship between literature and religion in Shakespeare's time. These studies are emphasizing how religion formed the matrix for discourse about love, politics, and ethics. Donna B. Hamilton puts it this way: "Religion during this period supplies the primary language of analysis."[8] Deborah Kuller Shuger defines religion as "a master code." Elizabethan culture is religious because religion lends validity to a broad array of themes—kingship, identity, rationality, language, marriage, and ethics. "They are not masked

5. In addition, see Knight, *Shakespeare and Religion*. Also *The Wheel of Fire* and *The Crown of Life*.

6. Battenhouse, *Shakespeare's Christian Dimension*.

7. See especially Milward, *Shakespeare's Religious Background*.

8. Hamilton, "Shakespeare and Religion," 189.

by religious discourse, but articulated in it; they are considered in relation to God and the human soul."[9] According to Shuger, gradual changes occurred in "habits of thought." These were the underlying structures of thought in and under the norms and values of that time. These transitions, however, do not weaken, they only alter, the character of that relationship.

The Religious Landscape

Elizabethan culture does not present us with a monolithic entity. That statement holds as well for the religious domain. Religious diversity characterized the era. In addition to the dissension between Roman Catholicism and Protestantism, these two wings of Christendom were beset with a host of differences among themselves. On the other hand, lying behind these varieties in religion one finds a common worldview—surely true when we speak about the English church. Donna Hamilton speaks to this when she refers to the view of the historian Collinson: "Most Protestants, Puritans and bishops alike, were bound together by a common theology and evangelical commitment and were determined to work together within the National Church to bring about reform at a popular level, to impose a new, disciplined, Protestant culture centered on the Word of God."[10]

Permit me to add an additional comment about the Elizabethan English religious landscape, in order to flesh out the situation a bit further. The unity of the medieval church had been lost, once and for all. Calvinism had been permitted in England during the reign of Henry VIII. This led to a unique form of Protestantism, the via media, later designated as the Church of England. After a woeful period, one which included the reign of a Mary other than Mary Tudor (1553–1558) who had launched a bloody suppression of Protestants, a period of consolidation ensued under Queen Elizabeth. She was the daughter of the marriage of Henry VIII and Anne Boleyn and ruled England for a long period, from 1558–1603. The Act of Uniformity was agreed to in 1559, by which the Book of Common Prayer (in the edition of 1552) was made obligatory for public worship. This Act of Uniformity was enforced by royal visitations. It was imposed and strongly reinforced by means of a catechism and homilies;

9. Shuger, *Habits of Thought in the English Renaissance*, 6.
10. Collinson, *The Religion of the Protestants*, 189.

these homilies included preaching on prescribed theological and social themes, which were strictly and regularly required to be read in public.

The way the Protestant impetus impinged on the populace was largely by means of the English language as found in the Great Bible of 1539, the Geneva Bible of 1560, the Bishop's Bible of 1568, the King James Bible of 1603, and the Book of Common Prayer. The Bible was taken up and assimilated by the citizens through preaching, proclamation, and personal readings. How deeply all these spiritual resources actually found lodging in the hearts of the church people is another question. According to Collinson, a Protestantism dominated by the prayer book came into being, which implied a measure of accommodation and was opposed to all kinds of radical representation on the part of the believers. This religious temper was also encouraged by the queen, who didn't like religious practices and testimonies of a radical and personal kind.

It was the Puritans who stressed the importance of just these practices and testimonies. The word *Puritan*, as is so often the case with such terms, was originally used more or less as a term to stigmatize the practitioners. In a later phase, it became a more precise term, as the group took the name for themselves. Followers of the Reformation, such as these, regarded the English Settlement as an incomplete reformation, one carried out only halfway. Apart from a few dissenters, they did not wish to separate themselves from the church. Still, they acted as a group apart from the established church.

The Roman Catholic belief community, of course, did not vanish all at once. The via media as designed by the state church had at heart that it would keep them on board—an outcome that proved successful in many cases.[11] There were, however, many pious priests among them who refused to commit themselves to the Anglican church. After 1570, they were called recusants. During the reign of Elizabeth, 123 priests were put to death. The influence of Roman Catholicism in the north remained great, practiced as it was by the nobility of the land. The great majority of the religious practitioners of the land, however, were comfortable with the new church order and law.

---

11. The English poet George Herbert describes it as "A fine aspect in fit array / neither too mean nor yet too gay."

Reticence

Shakespeare was heavily involved in this world. Apart from his plays we do not know with certainty anything about his attitude toward the Christian faith. We do know for certain that he knew his Bible well. To judge from the number of citations and references, he was more familiar with it than were his contemporaries. His literary sensitivity may well account for this familiarity with the Bible. Also certain, however, is that this familiarity was not only a matter of knowing some phrases from oral tradition; the truth is that he had read these himself.[12]

The quotations Shakespeare uses are derived almost exclusively from the Geneva Bible. Milward says as much when he writes: "There is hardly a book of the Old or the New Testament which is not represented at least by some chance word or phrase in one or other of his plays."[13] Milward correctly notes that Shakespeare's citations are not casual, incidental references, but are essential to the meaning of the play.

Next to the Biblical references, we find echoes of the Anglican liturgy and related homilies. Milward contends that there is clear proof of influence from the preaching of Henry Smith, called "Silver-Tongued Smith" by Thomas Nashe in *Pierce Penniless*.[14] Shakespeare's plays also display a wealth of theological knowledge. And he was well acquainted with the theological debates of the day, not only from the learned scholars, but also by involved laymen.[15] Reading between the lines, or, rather, through them, we can deduce which volatile theological issues people were occupying themselves with in his day. To surmise whether Shakespeare, by means of his plays, expressed his own opinion about the theological and ecclesiastical issues of the day is far more hazardous to venture. In a collection of essays entitled *Shakespeare and the Culture of Christianity in Early*

---

12. Cf. Noble, *Shakespeare's Biblical Knowledge*, and especially Shaheen's, *Biblical References in Shakespeare's Tragedies; Biblical References in Shakespeare's History Plays*; and *Biblical References in Shakespeare's Comedies*.

13. Milward, *Shakespeare's Religious Background*, 87.

14. "Whether they serve to prove, at least in their totality, a direct influence on the plays or not, they afford valuable illustrations of the religious context in which Shakespeare developed and enriched his themes" Milward, *Shakespeare's Religious Background*, 133.

15. Inter alia, Roland M. Frye, *Shakespeare and Christian Doctrine*. Frye holds fearlessly to his vision of Shakespeare's vital relation to Christendom.

Modern England,[16] various writers about Shakespeare have researched the possibility of ascertaining his own attitudes towards the Roman Catholic-Protestant controversy. Interpretations like these are interesting but at the same time highly questionable. John Freeman sees the ghost in Hamlet as a spirit emerging from the world of old Roman Catholicism that somehow meanders into the Elizabethan world.[17] The ghost is recognizable but not to be driven away, just as the Roman Catholic world is a permanent alternative to Protestant culture. Hamlet's "antic disposition" must be seen against the background of the strategies of the recusants. But according to Jennifer Rust, Hamlet portrays not the image of a Roman Catholic recusant, but of a Protestant sense of dread, of a man who had got loose from the older practicing rituals.[18] Consequently, man has embarked on a sea of uncertainty, with only Scripture as his compass and which he has to read without the help of tradition.[19]

These ingenious comments are rarely convincing. Such are my thoughts, and so their worth is very relative. It is tempting to invent a Protestant or Catholic Shakespeare, the more so when this Shakespeare agrees with one's own denomination, just as it is tempting to attribute all sorts of political opinions to Shakespeare. But these efforts, however perceptive they may be, will mostly display the ingenuity of the interpreter and will seldom convince the unprejudiced reader. Naturally, surprises are possible, but a certain amount of reticence is necessary toward all of these original discoveries which pretend to have found the real Shakespeare.

16. Taylor and Beauregard, *Shakespeare and the Culture of Christianity*.

17. Freeman, "This Side of Purgatory," 222–59.

18. Rust, "Wittenberg and Melancholic Allegory: The Reformation and its Discontent in *Hamlet*," in Taylor and Beauregard, *Shakespeare and the Culture of Christianity*.

19. Many examples exist of these wildly speculative interpretations. Watson, "*Othello* as Protestant Propaganda," 234–257, will have it that *Othello* was written against the background of the Protestant polemic against the Jesuits, and that Shakespeare is choosing sides. The flaw, then, of Othello is not only jealousy, but pride; he intends to win his beloved by works theological. He does not trust the evidences of Desdemona's love, who should be seen as an incarnation of the unearned and incomprehensible love of Christ. There are all kinds of expressions in *Othello* in which Watson hears references to an ongoing theological discussion. According to him, there is an "allegorical level of the play, where the marriage between Othello and Desdemona represents the precious but unstable marriage between the sinner's soul and its Savior" (235).

Other Influences

Naturally, other influences helped to shape Shakespeare's work. One such was the structural principle of humanism, another the impact of classical paganism—as transmitted to the England of the sixteenth century through the Italian Renaissance. In Shakespeare's day the classics sometimes served only as the literary model; sometimes, however, there is a real paganism, as is the case with Lorenzo Valla, who sees the heathen gods as personifications of human virtues.

One can trace in the works of Shakespeare his use of such models as Ovid, Seneca, Plautus, and Terence. Many of his works use a classical pagan setting. A customary practice of Shakespeare is to differentiate the main plot of his comedies, which follows classical protocol, from the more democratic subplot, in which often commentary about events in the main plot breathes a Christian spirit. In addition to the contributions of humanism, which draws on ancient literature, the spirit of Machiavellianism must be considered—even if it cannot be attributed to Machiavelli himself. We encounter the robust self-confidence of such a person, who relies on his own power and dexterity in his drive to satisfy his hunger for power, a goal for which he will overreach if necessary.

Furthermore, we must mention Stoical moral principles, especially the clear influence of Seneca. In a time of chaos, when the traditional institutions are eroding, the consolation that Stoicism offers provides some inner strength to the isolated person who finds himself in an uncertain world. Finding that assurance and the high-mindedness of his moral character in himself, he detaches himself from the fluctuating distractions that both good and bad people encounter in their lives.

We consider next the skepticism of Montaigne. In 1603 John Florio's edition of his essays appeared, though it may be that Shakespeare had seen copies in manuscript before this date. This skepticism is also a consequence of the discovery of new worlds outside Europe. Skepticism adopts a questioning attitude towards the universal meaning of European Christian morality.

These influences all mark a world in transition. The Renaissance is the era in which alternative interpretations of human nature and reality emerge. Both of these entities are now on their own, detached from their intrinsic relationship between God and his grace. These alternative explanations can take on the hue of Machiavellianism, Stoicism, or skepticism.

This new state of affairs can also be given a rationalistic interpretation, although the foundations for the rationalism of the seventeenth-century rationalism are not yet present. Rationalism and magic in the Renaissance run through each other and often form a remarkable amalgam. Sometimes these new mental attitudes generate an atheistic vision of life. Atheism is a repeated accusation in Shakespeare's world. Presumably in Shakespeare's adjoining neighborhood a group of men had organized themselves as "The School of Night"—authors such as Marlowe, Chapman, Mathew Royden, and John Heriot—with Sir Walter Raleigh as the central figure—and who were all suspected. Marlowe was accused of atheism and could exculpate himself only with great difficulty.

Roused by the development in the towns and the rise of the bourgeoisie, the European man took on in many respects a new self-confidence. He became a world citizen, a man living in a disordered but fascinating universe. Driven by the flywheel of commerce, he concentrated on the world and reflected on how he could exploit its possibilities. He became "a person of the world." The secular theater mirrored this transformation. As part of this development, the influence of Protestantism needs mentioning, which now did away with the distinction between the sacred and the profane. Deeper inner piety toned down an interest in holy times and places. Diligence in work and family life received a new emphasis in this mercantile world as the focus in which the true religion was to be experienced.[20]

To trace, as we have done, the various influences which shaped Shakespeare's work is not to say by any means that he is a spokesman for any of these influences, even less so that he represented all of them together. Many times he used them only for "stage purposes."[21] Shakespeare belongs to the modern era, but it is a popular misunderstanding to suppose that these currents of thought can be defined as a progressive emancipation from the Christian faith, or the Reformation reduced to a common denominator, or the baroque neatly defined. I have stated earlier that I see Shakespeare as one living in the modern era and as open to influences of the time in a complex and historical setting. I see him as one who composed marvelous works, which, in terms of content, whether deliberately or unconsciously, were inspired by the Bible and the basic

20. See inter alia Taylor, *Sources of the Self*, 211–33.
21. Eliot, "Shakespeare and the Stoicism of Seneca," in *Selected Essays*, 128.

tenets of Christendom, particularly those texts which Catholicism and Protestantism have in common.

How Do I Read Shakespeare?

We now need to draw conclusions about the matters we have considered in this chapter. I always keep a sharp focus on Shakespeare. How do I understand Shakespeare as a theologian? In my analysis I shall place particular attention to the way the Christian background shaped and worked its way into his plays. Without this recognition, his plays become unintelligible. The interaction between characters, the motives of the protagonists, the actions that they perform, and the management of the events cannot be understood from a non-Christian context.

All these constitute the preconditions for his plays. Those preconditions go beyond the formal context of the plays; their role is not merely decorative. I see Shakespeare's plays as part of the culture of a Christian era, certainly grounded in his time period, secular in form and content, but imbued with a Christian intuition. I boldly assert that the essentials of the Christian faith contributed to his plays and should be taken into account in any interpretation of his work. Whether or not I am correctly judging the intent of his plays will need to be determined from my analysis of his work. Any interpretation from a foreign point of view, one which is imposed on the text from without and leads to an artificial exegesis, needs to be rejected.

What I intend to say, however, is not only to demonstrate that a Christian influence pervades the plays, but also to show how his influence has a history of its own as an "incarnation" of a Christian worldview in the context of the modern era. I assert with some emphasis that there are different sources of inspiration in the work of Shakespeare. This Christian impetus does not operate in a purely neutral context. Its influence merges into "a field" of other influences. This is the only way creativity comes about. Besides this, one needs to acknowledge Shakespeare's heightened sensitivity towards his own day. Add to this genius and the imaginative power to shape experience and reality in dramatic form and appropriate language—and a genius is born. He has enlarged our sense of the world through his plays. This enlargement, as stated earlier, proceeds from a variety of sources, of which the Christian faith is a dominant one.

Interestingly, through this creative effort in the context of modernity, this Christian inspiration itself becomes enlarged. I do not intend to say by this enlargement that I expect all sorts of "new" theological insights, but, surely, it will lead to *originality and vibrance of thought*, which, by a process of enrichment and deepening, works on our understanding of the Christian man and his world and is, therefore, also relevant for theology.

From a theological point of view, this can also be stated: Christian belief is not to be reduced to a fixed set of dogmatic truths that, once formulated, remain fixed and static. It is a challenge for thoughts on life which have to be encountered time and again. The Christian faith is a creative model that makes forms of experience possible and, in turn, through experience, takes on flesh and blood. This process need not happen consciously. It is particularly in the artistic imagination that this process often occurs in a subconscious way.

Permit me to introduce one more issue—the so-called phenomenon of post-figuration. This is a derivation from pre-figuration. When we speak about foretelling in the theological sense we refer to what the Old Testament points in advance but also to other references which anticipate the Messiah, Jesus Christ.[22]

The fulfillment of these foreshadowings does not constitute the end of the story. After the fulfillment, there can be post-figurations, particularly in dramatic works. Whenever, within the context of a universe that bears the imprint of Christian belief, a play with a social or political setting is projected, a constellation is created. These constellations can become a transparency of the fundamental ur-drama, the Christian drama that is enacted between God and the world in and through the figure of Jesus Christ.

Drama in the context of the Christian faith will never transpire altogether outside the ur-drama—Christ. This ur-drama takes on, in the life of a Christian community, a key symbol, an original symbol, an archetype. It manifests itself when and wherever the artistic composition takes place in a certain horizon of belief and understanding. H. U. von Balthasar, in his impressive *Theo-Drama*, spells out the manner in which these post-figurations function. He says, "The connections . . . need not be made explicit no more than the poet needs to be aware of them. As a matter of course, this horizon is as fundamental for an objective understanding of

---

22. An authoritative study of this territory remains still that of Goppelt, *Typos*.

the play, as is the reality of Zeus and Apollo and the Eumenides in classical tragedies. But if men proceed to abstract this theological horizon and reduce it to the psychological analysis of a great character, it becomes inevitable that the drama will be misunderstood. Goethe and Hegel succumbed to this misinterpretation of Hamlet."[23] This post-figuration is not redundant after the play has happened. To quote Balthasar again: "No one who understands the acts of God can understand all the implications of being in Christ. It is the task of the Church and the world to disclose these implications, not systematically, but dramatically."[24]

Having said this, however, I do not intend to go the route of regarding Shakespeare's plays as allegories. They are "worldly" dramas, whose meaning and conclusion are self-contained. Nevertheless, these plays acquire greater meaning when we recognize how a basic ur-drama provides the underpinnings of a given play. Lacking living images from its own culture, Christ becomes a stranger in that culture; what ensues is a fatal division between the world of faith and our experiences in this world.

The ideas associated with post-figuration and their fulfillment is not to be forced. When they occur, we experience a moment of grace, a kairos moment in history. It is as if the characters are let loose on the stage, with a life independent of the poet. Such experiences have come to great writers, who also deferred to the role of the Holy Spirit. And the Holy Spirit generates recognizable and congenial artistry, words based on a poetical imagination, as flower-shaped designs appear on plain frozen glass, words influenced by original sources, in order to bring forth a new world in a different time and place.

23. Balthasar, *Theodramatic* I, 108.
24. Ibid.

1

The Merchant of Venice

OF SHAKESPEARE'S PLAYS, TEN are comedies. These engaging plays have held audiences spellbound from his time to ours. *The Comedy of Errors* is likely the first of the comedies; the last is *Twelfth Night*. They were written between 1584 and 1600.

The Plot

The Merchant of Venice relates how Antonio, a bachelor and rich merchant of Venice, is approached by his friend Bassanio for help. Bassanio wishes to try his luck in an affair involving the courtship of Portia, the daughter of a recently deceased noble from Belmont, a place Shakespeare defines vaguely as a place somewhere in dreamland. Antonio is prepared to make the funds available to Bassanio. Since his available capital at the moment, however, has been invested in a number of merchant ships, he has few readily available funds. For that reason he goes to Shylock, a Jew, who amasses his wealth by making loans at usurious rates of interest. Since Antonio finds this practice dishonorable, he makes no effort to conceal his disdain for Shylock. Shylock, in turn, harbors a strong dislike for Antonio. Still, he is willing to lend Antonio three thousand ducats, with the apparently frivolous stipulation that if Antonio does not return the loan within three months, Shylock will, as penalty, demand a pound of flesh from Antonio's body.

Bassanio sets out, accompanied by his lighthearted friend Gratiano. He is not the first to have risked this venture. Many suitors have preceded him, but to Portia's great relief, who had found them of little worth, they had all slunk away in disgrace. Portia's father had specified that whoever would win Portia must make a choice among three chests,

1

made, respectively, of gold, silver, and lead. A saying was attached to each chest, one that, superficially, at least, gave no clue as to which choice of chest would win Portia as wife. The act of choosing involves a risk, since the one who chooses wrongly must pledge to go through life unmarried. Obviously, the risk of the choice itself is also great. Two candidates nevertheless have just taken their chance. They chose, respectively, the gold and the silver chests and left Belmont disappointed. Now Bassanio makes his appearance. Portia is immediately attracted to him, and great is her pleasure when he makes the right choice—the leaden chest. Meanwhile, Gratiano has been busy seeking the hand of Portia's attendant, Nerissa.

Life in Venice has not been standing still this while. Lorenzo, one in Bassanio's group of friends, has unobtrusively, and in the blink of an eye, disguised Jessica and has made off with her to Belmont. Obviously, Shylock is raving mad, all the more so since she has taken a handsome dowry with her. But he receives new hope at news that Antonio's ships have met disasters on the high seas. True or not true, the consequence is inescapable: Antonio is unable to pay his loan by the designated day. Shylock now announces his intent to carry out the agreement set forth in the bond. Although the Venetians have never heard of such an arrangement, the duke is powerless to interfere with the agreement. Since the contract meets all the legal requirements, the statutory liability cannot be lightly dismissed.

When this news reaches Bassanio, he travels as quickly as possible to Venice. Without his knowledge, Portia and Nerissa follow him, arriving at the same time. As the alleged representative of a learned judge from Padua, she embraces the opportunity to preside over the case at hand. She acknowledges that, legally, Shylock has a sound case, but observes how far better it would be for everyone if he would permit justice to be tempered with mercy and, eventually, accept a monetary settlement as indemnification for the loan. Shylock will not hear of such measures. Alright, says the judge, so be it. But according to the letter of the law, as stated in the document, you have no right to so much as a drop of blood as you take Antonio's pound of flesh; moreover you must take exactly a pound of flesh, no more, and no less, under penalty of death.

Shylock shrinks back from the affair. But now the judge begins to turn the thumbscrews on the plaintiff. She reverses the procedures. A Venetian law stipulates that anyone who contrives harm against the life of another is to have his property seized and must plead for his very life.

And these acts of kindness cannot come into play unless he becomes a Christian; he is, moreover, to bequeath immediately half of his possessions to his daughter and the other half to the public domain. And now a hilarious bit that has been lying in wait closes the scene. Portia and Nerissa, still disguised as judge and clerk, coax their husbands, Bassanio and Gratiano, to return their wedding rings in gratitude for Portia's and Nerissa's services. This is the very ring that Bassanio has given Portia as a pledge for his faithfulness in marriage, and Gratiano's to Nerissa, Portia's assistant in the trial. One needs to wait until the end to see the resolution of this complication.

Meanwhile, news has arrived that Antonio's ships have met a far better fate than anyone could have predicted. The play ends in Belmont, the site where the favored ones pledge their marriage vows.

Shylock the Jew

Over the years, Shylock, the Jew, has received most of the attention in the play. And that is as it should be. Given his passionate outbursts, he is by far the most lively character of the play. Shylock, it is very clear, lives for money, having adopted the principle *Money breeds money* (1.3.91). He justifies his practice by appealing to Father Jacob, who used questionable tactics while breeding his flocks. Jacob and Laban agreed that the speckled offspring would devolve to Jacob , who then proceeded to exhibit wands before the eyes of the rams during mating season. This tactic supposedly generated speckled offspring, to Jacob's advantage. Shylock interprets this somewhat dubious practice, one that the interpreters of the Bible never condemned, as a shrewd procedure, comparable to the taking of interest on loans.

Shylock has elicited from his audiences expressions of human sympathy—maybe from Shakespeare himself—in the wake of the Jew's protests against the way he has become a target for resentment and cruelty. Obviously, Shakespeare has himself become enchanted by the character of Shylock. He has not altogether made up his mind about this character he designed for the play. Similarly, in *The Jew of Malta*, Marlowe's Jew harbors characteristics similar to Shylock's. Jews were arriving in England, but they had to walk warily if they wished to be tolerated.[1] Officially, Jews were to be deported under laws passed in England during the reign

1. See especially Shapiro, *Shakespeare and the Jews.*

of Edward I. Whether Shakespeare ever dealt with Jews is an intriguing question, but his generous spirit would surely have opened him up to sympathy for the alien. On the one hand, as we learn from other works, Shakespeare is not subject to xenophobia. It is possible that Shakespeare initially planned a comic figure who would be exposed to raillery from others, but then he began to be at war with himself. On the other hand, the author develops a flesh-and-blood character, one with deep problems and needs. Shakespeare was too great an author to reduce his characters to black and white schematics. Many examples exist of dual-natured characters who cause a tension in the onlookers by alternately attracting and repelling them. One thinks of Falstaff, who is far more comical than Shylock, and Caliban, in *The Tempest*, also an "outsider," a strange aboriginal with questionable character traits. Shylock, however, is a Jew not only aware of his race, but determined to display it and to preserve his identity:

> I will buy with you, sell with you,
> Talk with you, walk with you, and so following:
> But I will not eat with you, drink with you, nor pray with you
> (1.30ff).

As a Jew he desperately wishes to be integrated into partnership with the community. But he is in a quandary, forced as he is to consider the means of his livelihood. Because of the rule which forbids him to eat pork, he refuses to eat with the Christians. Nor will he pray with them. Owing to the very heart of his Jewish worship, he will remain perpetually an outsider. His identity as a Jew also conflicts with the masquerades which transpire in the town plaza. Here he is at one with the Puritans of Shakespeare's day. He scoffs at "the Christian fools with varnish'd faces" (2.5.33) and commands Jessica to keep her distance from these festivals.

Shylock's identity as a Jew is intimately bound up with his calling. This is the only way he can subsist. For that reason he interprets criticism of his calling as a criticism of his Jewishness, and he deals with these two givens as both identical and discrete.

Discrimination?

That Shylock feels he is a victim of discrimination, that he feels he is being treated like a dog, is abundantly clear. This attitude becomes obvious in his reaction to Antonio's request for a loan.

He hath disgrac'd me, and hind'red me half a million,
Laugh'd at my losses, mock'd at my gains,
Scorned my nation, thwarted my bargains,
Cooled my friends, heated mine enemies,
—And what's his reason?
I am a Jew (3.48ff).

What Shylock means is that Antonio has thwarted him in his calling, that by crossing him, Antonio has cost him a half million ducats—while all the while mocking him with his laughter. Antonio, he says, has defamed him and alienated him. Later he says:

Signior Antonio. many times and oft
in the Rialto you have rated me
About my moneys and my usances:
Still have I borne with a patient shrug,
(For suff'rance is the badge of all our tribe)
You call me misbeliever, cut-throat dog,
And spit upon my Jewish gabardine,
And all for use of that which is mine own (1.3.101ff).

The criticism about his conduct on the stock exchange he has borne, he says, with a patient shrug of the shoulders, for, as you know, patience is the identifying mark of our tribe. He has reviled me, calling me an unbeliever and bloodhound, and has spit on my Jewish garment. What is amiss with my calling? he asks. What is wrong with a legitimate use of one's goods—goods which another, in turn, is most eager to use?

All this is not to conclude that Antonio has drawn out the race card. Antonio's harshness towards Shylock concerns his behavior towards his debtors. One is hard put to find in the entire play a negative allegation about Jews. One instance of it, however, could be the statement of Solanio who describes the approach of Shylock's kinsman with these words: "Here comes another of the tribe: a third cannot be match'd, unless the devil himself turn Jew" (3.1.7ff).

But we also encounter contrasting attitudes. For example, Jessica, the daughter of Shylock, is described as a "most sweet Jew" (2.3.11). And when Shylock prepares to lend his ducats under the terms stipulated, Antonio will announce, for all to hear, "There is much kindness in the Jew" (1.2.149) and praises him as "gentle Jew" (173). It should not surprise us that a Jew is also defined as an *infidel*. This will grate on modern ears, but that word was being used to describe anyone who did not believe in God as the Christian church prescribed. Such a person was viewed as beyond the pale of salvation. This is, obviously, a mirror image of a Jew's attitude towards the Christians, since such a person refused to eat with Christians. One can hardly allege that discrimination is in play here if he uses the customary meaning of the word.

Shylock, then, lives in tension between his identity as a Jew and his secular calling. An attack against one involves an attack on the other. Could it be that Shylock is an early example of someone who greatly desires to use the argument of discrimination in order to find justification for his practice of acquiring wealth through his questionable practices? A distinction between the two is more difficult than it appears on first sight. The question that must finally be asked, in terms of the play, is this: How does it come about that he needs to sustain himself through acquiring wealth by means of interest? Has he not been so marginalized that he has been forced to earn his livelihood in this way? A sensitivity to this question is in order. I cannot believe that Shakespeare himself would fail to see this connection.

Another question. In his modeling of Shylock as a Jew who earns his livelihood by earning interest on loans, and is about to do so again, is it possible that Shakespeare, will yield, sometimes latently, sometimes more openly, to the anti-Semitism of his day? The characterization of a Jew as an unscrupulous miser who has designs on the life of the Christian Antonio could easily lead to a standard, negative reaction to all Jews. However, it is exactly because Shakespeare wishes to steer clear of the charge of current anti-Semitism that he assigns these malicious words to Shylock, and it is obvious that he was sufficiently sensitive to the temptation of expressing conventional attitudes that he would not himself give in to even an inch of it. What is more, one does well to remember that Shakespeare will present us later on with characters who likewise belong to a well-defined community. Such is the case with the play *Othello*. Othello, the Moor, is also an outsider, in Venice, who will play a fatal role. We meet the well-known Iago, a full Venetian, who, it turns out, is the real scoundrel. The effort is surely misplaced that holds up *The Merchant of Venice* as an exhibition of anti-Semitism.

Shylock as Critic

A question worth pursuing is this one: whether Shylock is intended to serve as a critical portrayal of the society of Shakespeare's day. Shylock, who endures criticism because of Antonio's outspoken description of him as merciless and hard-hearted, not only offers a robust defense, but goes on the offensive. Are you not guilty of the same charges which you lay against me? he asks. Are you not guilty of hypocrisy?

> Hath not a Jew eyes?
> Hath not a Jew hands, organs, dimensions, senses, affections, passions?
> Fed with the same food, hurt with the same weapons,
> Subject to the same diseases, healed by the same means,
> Warmed and cooled by the same winter and summer as a Christian is?
> If you prick us do we not bleed?
> If you tickle us do we not laugh?
> If you poison us do we not die?
> And if you wrong us shall we not revenge?
> If we are like you in the rest, we will resemble you in that.
> If a Jew wrong a Christian, what is his humility?
> Revenge!
> If a Christian wrong a Jew,
> what should his sufferance be by Christian example?
>
> Why, revenge! (3.1.53ff).

Should he be disposed to exercise revenge, says Shylock, he does not differ from the Christian. Jews and Christians partake of identical humanity; they have the same body and the same affections. He justifies his revenge by making it clear that no distinction can be made between him and them, for we measure each other by the same standards. He protests that if he sometimes appears to make exceptions in the conduct of his affairs, he remains still as much a human being as they are. Shylock is suggesting here that, in fact, revenge is a common human trait, and that discrimination occurs whenever men reproach him for what is common to mankind and accepted everywhere.

Shylock goes a step further in response to the reproach he is receiving for insisting on the payment of a pound of Antonio's flesh. How can you object to my claim when the same practice occurs in the Christian commonwealth?

> What judgment shall I dread doing no wrong?
> You have among you many a purchas'd slave,
> Which (like our asses, and your dogs and mules)
> You use in abject and slavish parts,
> Because you bought them,—shall I say to you,
> Let them be free, marry them to your heirs?
> You will answer
> The slaves are ours',—so do I answer you:
> The pound of flesh, which I demand of him
> Is dearly bought, 'tis mine and I will have it (4.1.89ff., 97ff).

The Christian world of Venice, that is to say, is well acquainted with slaves, who are regarded as property and used as animals. Do you rich folk ever free these slaves? No, of course not. They are understood to be your legal property. Where is that highly reputed love of mankind about which you Venetians boast so proudly? You deal in human beings and do with them whatever you please. What you buy is yours. Shylock has now bought a part of Antonio, and he is determined not to let the opportunity slip away from him.

Shylock surely makes a valid point here. *Corpus Christianum* advocates forgiveness but deals harshly. Shylock is the unfortunate outsider who is being shoved into a corner; he is not, however, without a defense. He can point out the inconsistencies of the Christian society. He can speak pointedly about the "hard dealings" of the Christians. Shylock is exposing the so-called Christian society of Venice. His purpose is not to advocate a reform of this society but to justify the hazardous road on which he has ventured. Recall once more that Shylock's real problem has nothing to do with his Jewishness. Earlier we spoke about the predatory spirit of capitalism, which appears here already in an early form. One can always find people who even with their eyes wide open fall into the same logical trap into which Shylock has fallen. They see *The Merchant of Venice* only as a problem play in which some dominant citizens display their fear and contempt for outsiders.

Shakespeare has no intention of permitting the force of his play to hinge on the intention of the Jew to strike a blow at his enemies or to lecture the Venetian society—who obviously have their counterparts in London. It is possible to take up the cause of the lighthearted characters as a gesture of affirming modern sensibilities. Shylock is a living figure who justly demands attention from the spectator or reader for his argument. He defends his reasoning and his cause, and by doing so he calls for a recognition of his Jewish identity and Jewish law in contrast to the prevailing attitudes towards humanity in Venice as well as Venetian law. But one must not lose sight of the fact that he is a usurer, for whom procuring wealth is the highest good. He knows well that his best defense is to accuse a Christian of hard-heartedness (where he surely has a point) whereas he, in fact, has a problem understanding their kindness. He is not continuously unsympathetic, for each party understands that they are all trying to survive in their calling—granted the dissimilarities—and also so that he can ply and charm with his own brand of humor to display the resources of his culture. Shakespeare has keen insight into the psyche of a survivor who lives by his wits and, when necessary, by his cunning. There are limits, however, and they are being approached every time Shylock carries on about his right to thrust his knife into Antonio's body. The boundaries between right and wrong are fluid, and God lets his light shine even on such an old miser as Shylock. The reader or spectator may well enjoy Shylock's performance, and though it may then occur to him that there is a lesser distinction between him and Shylock than he pretends, the distinction nevertheless between the comic and the serious now becomes stretched. Shylock reveals himself before the learned judge as a bloodthirsty creature who crosses the line and intends with impunity to end the life of a fellow citizen. Now we need to suppress the laughter on our lips as it becomes obvious that miserliness and greediness are very dangerous traits. The dramatic high point occurs when Shylock proceeds to whet his knife on the sole of his shoe, and when Gratiano, in the company of Bassanio, says to him:

> Not on thy sole: but on the soul (harsh Jew)
> Thou mak'st thy knife keen; but no metal can,—
> No, not the hangman's axe—bear half the keenness
> Of thy sharp envy; can no prayers pierce thee? (4.1.123ff).

Shylock, says Gratiano, is sharpening his knife on his own soul, so that his envy becomes all the keener. He is accused of harboring a wolfish nature because of his passionate thirst, his famished and rapacious appetite for blood. At any moment Portia, in her role as judge, will reverse the proceedings and tighten the screws as the court proceeds to bring a closure to the case—including an earlier issue that occurred in Venice and of which the duke is aware. She asks whether he, Shylock, has at least arranged for a doctor, to prevent Antonio from bleeding to death. He does not suppose this is necessary, for the contract, literally speaking, says nothing about a doctor. It now becomes highly obvious that Shylock wishes only to run Antonio through with a knife. But now the contract will be even more strictly enforced, and Shylock will depart "with a flea in his ear" (*kous op de kop*). For anyone to protest now against the proceedings as displaying callousness is to betray sentimentality and an undeveloped sense of justice.

All this is not to say that the outcome of the process is wholly satisfying. Shylock draws in his horns and slinks off. Seldom does one find an exit so anticlimactic. Shakespeare can deal harshly with his characters. He will do the same with Falstaff, who is made to die offstage. This bone sticks in the throat of many readers. *The Merchant of Venice* is a comedy with some painful features. Comedies are intended to induce laughter, but one play can arouse deep-down laughter more than another.

Antonio

The Merchant of Venice embodies a variety of themes. It is a play with a happy ending, since in the last scene three sets of lovers pair off into a moonlight mist, where one can suppose the sonata one hears is the music of the spheres. Since all comedies turn, finally, on love and loss of one's heart to another, the characters move out to Belmont and get married, honorably and in good faith. At the same time, the play has moral points to make. The scene involving the three caskets, for example, teaches the spectator to look beyond the surface of things. Did the unfortunate Moor not discover the truth that "all that glisters is not gold" after reading the text and coming up empty-handed after he chooses the gold chest?

If we are to understand the central theme of the play, however, we need to examine Antonio—the character, by the way, after whom the play was carelessly named. We find him at the very beginning of the play in a melancholy state of mind. The source of his melancholy, however, is not very clear—though it is so pervasive that, despite the fortunate turn of his ventures, he imparts a tone of melancholy to the entire play. Antonio now agrees to lend Bassanio the wherewithal necessary to test his luck in the Belmont venture. He is prepared, moreover, to borrow the money on Shylock's terms—distasteful though he finds it to deal with Shylock. Indeed, the affair is dubious, but his motives are honorable. This is the first encounter between Shylock and Antonio, but it foreshadows the high drama of later scenes.

Interest and Usury

A debate ensues between Antonio and Shylock over the moral legitimacy of interest (1.3.66–97).[2] As was pointed out earlier, Shylock brings up the example of Jacob, who tricked Laban into agreeing to let him hold up wands before his flocks at the time of breeding. In this way, says Shylock, he multiplied his flocks. Shylock further implies that Jacob treated Laban not as a fellow Israelite, but as an alien. According to Deuteronomy 23:20–21, an Israelite was not permitted to take interest from a fellow citizen, but could do so from an alien. Since Shylock himself lacks the three thousand ducats for the loan, he is permitted to borrow that sum from Tubal ("a wealthy Hebrew of my tribe") interest-free. Antonio challenges him. Did you not bring up this matter of Jacob to justify the taking of interest, and are goats and rams to be compared with gold and silver? As an aside to Bassanio, he points out that even the devil can cite Scripture to suit his purpose. The conclusion could not be clearer. There is no biblical basis for taking of interest, let alone usury.

Shakespeare's England was nervous about the question of interest. The official position was that, because of the grief and injustices to which it leads, the practice of taking interest was to be frowned upon. At the same time, it was conceded that it is impossible to forbid the practice outright. Francis Bacon says as much in the *Essays*. Interest given for commercial purposes, for a reasonable and regulated rate, should be permitted, though he allows this only as a concession in this Latin citation: *propter duritiem cordis* (a concession made necessary for the hardness of the heart).[3] In Shakespeare's time a distinction was made between lending for a commercial arrangement, whereby one can approve the form of interest as legitimate, and a loan designed for noncommercial purposes. Antonio's loan to Bassanio falls into the latter category.[4]

In the Calvinistic branch of the Reformation the legitimacy of interest was never called into question. Calvin is very clear about this.[5] To be

---

2. Kermode also designates this theme as central. See "Our Muddy Vesture," 17.

3. Bacon, *A Selection of his Works*, 152. The essay was published in 1625.

4. See, in addition, Kish-Goodling, "Using *The Merchant of Venice* in Teaching Monetary Economics," 330–39.

5. "Is it lawful to make money by renting a piece of ground, yet unlawful to make it from money? What?" John Calvin, *Letters of Advice* 6.1 *(On Usury)*, in O'Donovan and Lockwood O'Donovan, *From Irenaeus to Grotius: A Sourcebook in Christian Political Thought*, 683.

sure, he bases his consent to this practice on the principles of common humanity. Moreover, he finds making one's livelihood by pursuing interest unseemly. William Perkins (1558–1602), the influential theologian, touches indirectly on this point in his *A Treatise of Christian Equity*. He does not forbid interest but urges one to follow legal principles. The law also adds that one is not to punish the debtor to the extremes, to the maximum of the stated terms. A man, after all, "observes public equity when he dealeth not with his neighbor according to that extremity which the strict words of the law will bear, but according to that moderation which good conscience requireth."[6] A person who wishes to act justly will not squeeze someone into a tiny corner—a tactic that the law may allow—but will take thought of his fellow man, tempering his demands according to the spirit of the law. I am strongly convinced that the key to understanding *The Merchant of Venice* lies right here. The issue is not about some fine point concerning the legitimacy of receiving interest. It is really about this question: In what spirit are we to interpret the letter of the law? Naturally, Shylock is entitled to earn interest on his loan, and he may do it in his own way, but when he detaches his affair from a concern for humanity, then something has gone radically amiss. The letter of the law can lead to gross injustice; "the laws of men are polity, but equity is Christianity" (Perkins). The written law as well as the relationships involved in a contract are political matters, but fairness and equity is Christlike, and the laws must be interpreted in the light of this rule. Much of the talk encourages moderation, so that the alternative—severe injury to Antonio—may be avoided.

Antonio has not made clear to Shylock his dislike of the practice of usury nor persuaded him to soften his demands. In setting his rates, Shylock has exceeded the prevailing rate allowed. At the same time, he remains unrelenting in his demands—shows no willingness to budge an inch—as the date approaches. Usury is rent without moderation, a practice which leads to drastic extremes.

Liberality

The play achieves even greater depth when the interesting theological issue of liberality, or generosity, is introduced. In this matter, Antonio's attitude is directly opposite that of Shylock's. Antonio is liberal, generous.

6. In O'Donovan and Lockwood O'Donovan, *From Irenaeus to Grotius: A Sourcebook in Christian Political Thought*, 776.

He was that earlier already, before he was squeezed into this narrow corner through Shylock's machinations.

> I oft deliver'd from his forfeitures
> Many that have at times made moan to me (3.3.22ff).

Thus, we see that Antonio had rescued folk in a time of their need. And he is not the only one who displays a generous heart. Bassanio is of the same mind, ready to give up everything, life itself, and all the world, "aye sacrifice them all" (4.1.280, 282), in order to rescue Antonio from Shylock's clutches. Portia is imbued with the same spirit of liberality.[7] She places everything she owns at Bassanio's disposal. When she learns about Antonio's desperate situation, she foregoes the rituals of her wedding night and directs Bassanio to accompany Antonio and be prepared to pay six thousand ducats. This gesture of liberality is prompted by love and deep affection.

Liberality in *The Merchant of Venice* thrives in an ambience where people are not only willing to take leave of their possessions, but also to display deep trust. One who truly gives does so without a guarantee to repayment. Liberality, thus, is conditional on a readiness by the friend to take risks. Antonio as merchant is not a stranger to such arrangements. Indeed, Antonio's ships may sink to the bottom of the sea. This risk is not to be regarded as a necessary evil, but it allows room for the exercise of "the hand of heaven" (1.3.88). When Antonio lends the money, he is also prepared to risk his very life, however improbable that outcome initially appears.

This theme, liberality, plays out in another scene, in an emphatic way. Bassanio chooses the casket with the inscription "Who chooseth me, must give and hazard all he hath" (2.7.16). The aspirants who preceded him had played it safe. Their love for Portia had an eye for commercial advantage, and to "hazard for lead" was asking too much. Bassanio alone is willing to take this risk. Here lies the power of his love, that he exposes himself to all the consequences of his risk. In the meantime, the same thing is happening in Venice. Jessica, the Jewess, chooses to wed the Venetian Lorenzo, wholly against the will of her father. Jessica's decision to

---

7. A notable negative portrayal of Portia is that of Woldring, *Westerse waarden door Shakespeare belicht*, 149–69. She is accused of hypocrisy, which certainly goes too far. Woldring would have it that *The Merchant of Venice* is a tragedy, with Shylock as the tragic figure, a notion obviously motivated by modern sensibility.

obey the prompting of her heart involves a high risk, though one must also point out that this risk is somewhat offset for, in fact, they appropriate a tidy sum from Shylock's home for travel expenses.

Dramatic conventions in comedy call for attention to love, along with all that accompanies the theme. It includes the erotic (with some bawdiness comprising a subplot) and gives it full play. And this issue must not be downplayed, but given its full due. *The Merchant of Venice* is no exception to this convention. It deals with the theme of love forthrightly. The bantering about love transpires in a context in which the characters make hints about limits via sexual innuendos. In this context the Venetians constitute another contrast with Shylock. He orders Jessica: "Lock up my doors" (2.5.29) and is devastated when it becomes evident that she has escaped. It is probable that, as suggested earlier, Shakespeare is holding up to ridicule the strict Puritan attitudes whenever he has Shylock express his distaste for the masque and for feasts, and describes his own house as "a sober house."[8] And he trivializes the nature of love when he grieves the loss of a ring that goes back to his bachelor days, a ring that his wife Leah (now deceased) had given him. Moreover, we see how the spirit of love opposes the spirit of gold, how the spirit of generosity opposes the spirit of acquisitiveness, and how the spirit of adventure and risk opposes the spirit of safety and security.

The liberality being discussed here, however, is not to be confused with wasteful squandering. In his play *Timon of Athens* Shakespeare has demonstrated the results of unbridled generosity. In that play he riddles that practice with bullets, and it is not surprising that the unbounded friendship of Timon results in open misanthropy. Surely the context of love and erotic bantering requires and depends on generosity and open-handedness, circumscribed and appropriately restrained. It is not a flippant comment with which Gratiano ends the play—a double entendre, really:

> Well, while I live, I'll fear no other thing
> So sore, as keeping safe Nerissa's ring (5.1.306ff)

---

8. Velma Bourgeois Richmond attempts to read the play as containing a concealed agenda involving the contrast between Roman Catholicism and Protestantism. She contends that Shakespeare is expressing Roman Catholic sympathies. See *Shakespeare, Catholicism and Romance*, 121–8. She belabors the similarities between the Jews and the Puritans.

The episode of the ring at the end of the play makes it abundantly clear that liberality is a virtue only when the gift that is given is cherished. The one who practices liberality beyond proper limits of mutual trust is setting himself up for a deterioration of relationships. Although Bassanio and Gratiano for that reason had no right to give away their rings, they did so to "pour out" their deep gratitude. No single virtue exists all by itself, and when one virtue claims the entire field, it will easily become transformed into a vice. Viewed in this way, Shylock is justified in complaining that the costly ring, which embedded a turquoise stone, a ring which he had received from his wife (she has died prior to the time of the play), is exchanged by his daughter for an ape (3.1.108). He laments, to be sure, the loss of goods more than the loss of a priceless remembrance, but it becomes obvious that he is diminishing the status of human beings, as he so shrilly ranks nonhuman objects as higher than human ones, in his talk about procuring a similar ring in exchange for an ape. The ring on his hand from his beloved, therefore, does him little good. Liberality requires that the ring on the finger be accepted in trust; this symbol is not to be trifled with.

The Basis of the Ethics of Liberality

The basis of liberality, and with that the high esteem bestowed on the loved one, form the kernel of what is meant by being "Christlike"—as the play describes it. Better said, life as it unfolds in Venice and Belmont has Christian underpinnings. This may be less than obvious. Are we not concerned with a set of virtues which are *sui generic*, self-vindicated, and that need no further basis? To say so is to have a superficial view of the matter. In *The Merchant of Venice* the ground for liberality becomes evident in Portia's pleadings. She tries to persuade Shylock that it is better to give than to receive and that renouncing a formal judicially acknowledged right, in the interest of the other, has its roots in divinity itself. Robed as a learned judge, Portia puts out a call for mercy. Mercy is not a virtue that can be wrung, or forced:

> The quality of mercy is not strain'd,
> It droppeth as the gentle rain from heaven
> Upon the place beneath; it is twice blest,
> It blesseth him that gives and him that takes (4.1.180ff).

The source of grace, viewed as "an attribute to God himself," including the proposed acquittal, forgiveness, lies in the heavens. He is the God who goes beyond justice, for without such a God no man would achieve salvation (4.1.196). As human beings we stand in the presence of God as guilty sinners who need to beg for grace, as we also seek forgiveness from each other. The one who insists on the letter of the law and claims to be a just person is placing his eternal weal at risk.

> Consider this,
> That in the course of justice, none of us
> Should see salvation (4.1.194ff).

For these reasons Shylock is called upon "to mitigate the justice of thy plea." Such moderation would signal his readiness to settle for less than he is entitled to and thereby show regard for the other. This comes at the request of the other, but should also flow from oneself. The unrepentant one will not only forfeit access to God's mercy; in this life the soul will become as hard as the stone on which one sharpens his knife in order to perpetrate evil against another ("On my soul (harsh Jew), thou mak'st thy knife keen").

But Shylock is of a wholly other mind. It is just possible that Shakespeare's understanding of making peace falls short of acknowledging the true character of God in the way he places a one-sided emphasis on God's righteousness; however that may be, that theme does not get expressed in the play. He also proposes another mindset in society, one in which people are to relate in a different way to each other. They are captured by the incestuous drive to increase their wealth, in the spirit of *money breeds money*. It is the spirit of the contract, which pounds its fists on the table demanding the letter of the law in order to wring the maximum advantage from his relationship to the other. Wealth acquired in this manner opens no opportunity for friendship, love, or grace. A community that thrives on relationships based on gold is compelled to ask the question whether money remains a servant of humanity or whether money has such power that while it increases wealth it does so in a world that keeps shrinking. Since money has such power, it is necessary to offer strong opposition to it.

Antonio is repelled by the spirit of usury. His distaste for these practices will obviously combine with dubious thoughts of anti-Semitism and will open him up to charges of xenophobia. Anyone who can advance such an interpretation when engaged with such a straightforward and felicitously composed work is overlooking the text and is transforming it into one about Antonio's lies. The kernel of the play, however, eschews the spirit of greed, for greed leads to a calloused heart alongside the attitude which diminishes humanity in relationship to wealth.

Secularization?

An important question arises when we study other plays of Shakespeare. It is this: In how far are his notions anchored in a giving and forgiving God, a God who must be seen as the ultimate source and fountain of these attributes? Or is Shakespeare simply using traditional terminology—but words with meanings altered from their original source as they undergo a process of secularization and as they acquire a more worldly application loosed from their religious roots? Put it another way. Are the references to God, love of mankind, and grace, used in their fundamental sense or are they gradually losing force in the ongoing development of Western culture and of the life of society, and are such words, then, losing their power and significance?

It is not easy to make a decision about *The Merchant of Venice* in these matters. What is unmistakably clear is that the opposition against usury (and to a lesser extent, interest) should greatly concern the churches based as it is on a Christian worldview. It is also undeniable that life flourishes in an ambience of generosity and openness—attitudes that provide opportunities for one's life and are also hospitable to the preaching of the Gospel. One can also promote attitudes which can nurture plays about love.

The values we are discussing, however, are vulnerable. In a society where commerce flourishes, wealth itself can become the goal of the activities. The merchant and the banker merge into a one-two relationship in which everything turns on the multiplication of wealth. The enormous temptation that such commerce provides can, thus, lead to a hardening of the heart alongside the clinking of the coins. Money becomes an end in itself, severed from personal relationships, initiatives, liberality, and friendship. Can the financial world ultimately exist detached from "commerce" between God and man—realities that ultimately flow from God's own generosity and is intended to reflect itself in human affairs?

But love can also deteriorate. Will it be able to maintain its openness and generosity? Will its spirit of liberality remain alive? Love can be reduced to calculation. The competitors of Bassanio trip over these matters. Still another hazard is the possible breakup of the bonds of love in marriage—a risk which dogs Bassanio and Gratiano. The ring given by the beloved is not to be besmirched. The freely-given "Yes" is a word which involves risk and demands the integrity on the part of her who gives it. There can be no eros with agape if the mutual commitment of the lover is not to wither or be frittered away.

Conclusion

It can be protested that the play is "te zwaar" (too heavy) for a comedy. Or that the melancholy of Antonio does not comport well for a comedy. Perhaps these features can prompt us to categorize the play more as a problem play, such as *Measure for Measure*. But comedy for Shakespeare is an open form. In his other comedies Shakespeare also introduces serious problems within the customary conventions of comedy. This is surely the case in his last comedy, *Twelfth Night*. *The Merchant of Venice* undeniably embraces discordant elements. What probably happened is that Shakespeare planned to compose a comedy based on his sources, but that as he proceeded with the narrative, he kept his mind open to introducing heavier themes than he originally intended. The problem of interest is, finally, no trivial matter. Is it not true that a community that severs itself from mercy and generosity, from friendship and liberality, is a community in which men sustain an unnatural relationship to each other? *The Merchant of Venice* is an engaging work, one that centers on the romantic love between Bassanio and Portia and, in subplots, between Lorenzo and Jessica and between Gratiano and Nerissa. But it is also a serious play, one that provides much to enjoy as well as to think about.

2

King Richard II

THE FIRST PLAY THAT Shakespeare wrote is a so-called historical play, *King Henry VI, Part One*. For a dramatist it is no simple undertaking to examine the historical chronicles available to him and compose a play in which not only is the narrative comprehensible but the final states of the characters are as they should be. Shakespeare matured quickly in his mastery of this genre—one of the few successful writers in raising history plays to the level of high art.

King Richard II, the subject of this essay, constitutes the first play in a tetralogy. Shakespeare had, in fact, written an earlier tetralogy. The plays in that group consist of *Henry VI, Part 1; Part 2;* and *Part 3*, along with *King Richard III*. With *Richard II* we begin a second series, one which also includes *King Henry IV, Part 1* and *Part 2* and *King Henry V*.[1] The time covered in the second tetralogy actually precedes the action of the first tetralogy. The sequence of the kings is as follows: Richard II, Henry IV, Henry V, Henry VI, (Edward IV), Richard III, and Henry VII. The plays portray the history of most of the fifteenth century (Richard II became king in 1381; Henry VII came into power in 1485).

From a literary point of view, *Richard II* cannot be regarded as the greatest of these dramatic achievements. That distinction is reserved for *King Henry IV, Part 1*, not least for the role of the unique character Falstaff. Nevertheless, *Richard II* occupies a key role in both tetralogies. One can say that the deposition of the divinely appointed Richard II, later murdered, constitutes the initial event about which all subsequent action transpires. The reigns of Henry IV, Henry V, and Henry VI are all affected negatively from the desecration of the throne through Richard's

---

1. Shakespeare wrote *King John* between the two tetralogies. The play deals with a king who ruled in the beginning of the thirteenth century.

deposition. Even with King Richard III does the violation of the rules of succession barely get resolved. Although Richard III is himself a scoundrel (a familiar type derived from the medieval dramatic tradition), he is God's scourge, by whom God executes judgment. As later action develops, the scourge is mitigated, and the opportunity for a new beginning presents itself. Henry VII is a good king, who unites the royal houses of the Plantagenets (the Richard line) and the Lancastrian (the Henry line).[2]

It is not accidental that Shakespeare has given us ten history plays—among them, the two tetralogies.[3] England was experiencing a strong surge of national awareness in the sixteenth century. This phenomenon becomes apparent in the numerous writers of chronicles, among whom Holinshed was the most important.[4] Shakespeare's history plays are based on these chronicles, especially on the work of Holinshed, already named. This historian sets his account in the category of providential governance. In his telling, the hand of God is clearly at work as the one who directs history. With the great majority of Elizabethans, Shakespeare embraces this point of view. It represents a perspective of history which serves as an alternate model to that of "Machiavellianism." The latter model is, in fact, a secularized vision of history, in which history is defined by the deeds of the individual, who pursues his ends and purposes and, when successful, enhances his power. Shakespeare subscribes to the vision of a governing providence in history.[5] This appears in the relationship between actions and guilt and the consequences of that guilt upon later generations. This vision of history is the one I will be implicitly endorsing in my interpretation of *Richard II*.

The Narrative

Richard II is grandson of King Edward III (the oldest son, the Black Prince, is already dead). Another son of Edward III is Gloucester. He has been murdered (this has taken place before the time with which *Richard II* begins), and suspicions are abroad that Richard himself was involved

---

2. "We will unite the white rose and the red" (*Richard III*, 5. 5.19).

3. Shakespeare wrote still another play after the so-called tetralogies and *King John*, namely, *King Henry VIII*, Shakespeare's last play. It is apparently a co-authored work.

4. England, along with France, was one of the first nations in which a form of national consciousness makes its appearance.

5. Cf. especially Tillyard, *Shakespeare's History's Plays*.

in his death. Another son of Edward III is John of Gaunt, who is still alive at the beginning of the play. John of Gaunt has a son, Henry Bolingbroke, "the coming man," the one who will wrest the throne from Richard II.

Richard II, broadly speaking, divides into four parts. In the first part, Richard as king gives a favorable impression. He settles with skill an argument between prominent nobles, both of whom have been accused of treason. One of these is called Henry Bolingbroke, his nephew; the other is Thomas Mowbray. Both are banished from the land, although the sentence of Bolingbroke, through the pleadings of Gaunt, is reduced to six years. In the second part, Richard turns out to be a tyrannical king. He calls on the dying Gaunt, who has lectured Richard on his misgovernment. Richard has surrounded himself with flatterers, much to his hurt. Richard responds with unwonted cynicism, and when Gaunt dies, he confiscates his possessions. Richard badly needs this money in order to conduct a campaign against the rebelling Irish. Owing to an extravagant lifestyle, the public treasury is empty. With the confiscation of his father's goods, Bolingbroke, however, has been deprived of his inheritance. This is a fatal step. For many of the nobles, the measure of their grievances is full. As Bolingbroke lands in England (since the term of his banishment has expired, and because his property has been confiscated), he is joined by other nobles.

Meanwhile, Richard has gone to Ireland, and, as he learns about Bolingbroke's return, he understands that this is an act of rebellion. With this, the third part of the play begins. At first he remains fairly optimistic, but it soon appears that the basis of his support has dwindled. When an army of Welshmen on whom he had counted for support hears of rumors that the king is dead, they abandon him. The common people take the side of Bolingbroke (the high taxes have not made Richard popular), and the vice-regent of York (also a son of Edward III) on whom Richard has set his hope, takes a neutral position. Because of these flagrant crimes, a number of fine nobles who had formerly sympathized with Richard and who saw the injustice inflicted against Bolingbroke as a signal of further infringements on their privileges, also choose for Bolingbroke.

With this begins part four, the drama itself. The authority of Richard slowly diminishes, and however Bolingbroke repeatedly declares that his only goal is to have his rights restored, his actions, as they proceed, steer in the direction of higher ambitions. Richard has finally distanced himself from his royal dignity. His protectors are killed, his wife has been sent back to France, and Richard himself is finally imprisoned in Pomfret, in Yorkshire. There he is murdered. Despite the suggestions that Bolingbroke had been involved in the murder, he firmly denies such involvement.

Richard II as King

The tragic figure of Richard II occupies the center of the action in the play. Indeed, the official title of the play is *Richard II*. God's anointed he may be, but he contrives to lose both his power and his title. The play derives its unique profile and depth through the expression of his reactions to his predicament. He represents one of the most famous examples[6] in the dramatic tradition of the theme of "uncrowning of the king."[7]

Of course, tragedies, by definition, always involve the fall of a king or other highly placed individuals. This is surely the case with classical tragedies, but in Christian Europe it has never been otherwise. One counterpart must be mentioned. Adam was not literally a king (looking away from Christ), his calling being that of a gardener, as in *Hamlet*, a play that includes men with spades as gravediggers.[8] But though a landlord, Adam is also the progenitor of the human race and naturally occupies a place of honor. Well known also is *Paradise Lost*, by John Milton, a tragedy based upon the fall of Adam. And here Adam is named a king. He is the royal person whose calling is to rule over all things. That kingly role, however, is not an office that he derived from nature, but a prerogative granted from God himself. Adam lost his kingdom through a mistaken use of this position.

Dramas about kings embody an intrinsic value. The theme of kingship in the England of Shakespeare's day was a serious issue. The king is God's anointed one, a visible reminder of the sacred character of political reality. The sacred dimension of the Commonwealth is expressed very effectively by Ulysses in *Troilus and Cressida*:

> There is a mystery (with whom relation
> Durst never meddle) in the soul of state

---

6. The foremost example is that of King Lear. In a strict sense, however, he was not uncrowned, since he abdicated voluntarily.

7. See also, inter alia, Balthasar, *Theodramatic* I, 375–82.

8. See *Hamlet* 5.1.25ff. Cf. also the "thou, old Adam's likeness," spoken to the gardener in *Richard II* itself (3.4.73).

Which hath an operation more divine
Than breath or pen can give expression to (3.3.203ff).[9]

The well-being of the commonwealth is of the utmost importance, and its fate depends on the king. That truth will become only more obvious during the formation of national states. The legitimacy of the crown is no longer dependent upon the Pope (Shakespeare deals with this issue in *King John*), but that does not imply that the state is lacking divine sanction. The crown is carried over through the law of succession. God may appoint whomever he wishes as king, but he works through the institution of succession. The monarchy was a highly debated issue during the Renaissance, and there were fellows who made the case for a republic. The debate goes back to classical precedents (the spirit of republicanism is given a strong voice in *Julius Caesar*) among others, so that succession through arbitrary means can become apparent. There was, besides, a real reason for the interest in monarchy. Queen Elizabeth ruled during Shakespeare's time. She did so, to be sure, with the help of her ministers, and she relied heavily on Parliament as well. She was able to bring a strong measure of stability in the land, after a period of turbulence. This stability did not, however, go unchallenged. What is more, with a virgin queen as a monarch, the problem of succession naturally became a burning issue.

The political relevance of Shakespeare's history plays does not imply that they must be read as political allegories. Naturally, Shakespeare would not have been insensitive to the actual political situation of his time and would have referred to these realities, though "under the skin." Without isolating himself from his world, he nevertheless, also for self-preservation, kept the actual political world at a distance.[10] For a dramatist to make direct allusions to situations that involved the royal court was to risk censorship of the play or, worse, to arouse the suspicion that a group of dramatists was arrayed as enemies against the king. Nor should one look too diligently for trivial messages directed at the court in such a work as *Richard II*.

One can, nevertheless, say that these political plays convey a universal human significance. The king is the man *par excellence*. A true tragedy

9. That is, the sacred character of the state is not to be enfeebled by rational examination.

10. There is no denying that Shakespeare's plays had an effect in the political domain. Notable is the pronouncement of Queen Elizabeth: "I am Richard II," a comment that surely shows Shakespeare's influence.

demands a great figure, and who is greater than the king? This king does not live unto himself, but finds himself as part of a metaphysical framework. He is an ambassador of God, and without an acknowledgement of this "mythical" reality, one will find the entire situation incomprehensible. The luster of the king, however, glances off every man. The fate of the king is not separable from that of each person. For that reason the fall of a king is not only a spectacle for an interested observer of the political scene (and who in the ancient polis and in the time of developing monarchies was not such an observer?), but it is also valid for all: *tua res agitur.* Your own fate is involved. It is clear, thus, on the one hand, that not just any man is a king. The political reality is that of a hierarchy, and the king stands, alone, at the very top. One does not find in Shakespeare any concession towards a democratic leveling. A revolt of the masses is not only a misadventure doomed to fail, but also detrimental for the human community.[11]

On the other hand, Christian Europe was committed to a high regard for human dignity. Man is a son of Adam, redeemed through Jesus Christ, who confers on him the rank of king. This democratization of Christendom served to make the king a projection of every man. It is this mirroring of every man by the king that lends deeper significance to the play than only the fate of a deposed king.[12]

Richard the Failing King

Richard is the failing king. Although at first the play presents him as a qualified ruler, when he *ex officio* settles an altercation between Mowbray and Bolingbroke, it becomes rapidly apparent that outside his official and theatrical roles, his behavior raises serious doubts. This becomes clear in his meeting with Gaunt, on his deathbed, who, before Richard's arrival, pronounces a eulogy about England, lines that have made the heart of many a patriot beat faster. England,

> Whose rocky shore beats back the envious siege
> Of wat'ry Neptune, is now bound in with shame,
> With inky blots and rotten parchment bonds (2.1.62ff).

11. Shakespeare here has in mind, among others, the figure of Jack Cade, a notorious revolutionary.

12. This applies as well to Shakespeare's tragedies, especially *King Lear*.

Alas, he is saying, this proud England, this free land, encircled by the sea, which has succeeded in holding out against watery Neptune's mighty assaults, is now the slave of "inky blots and rotten parchment bonds" that report the sale of the royal estates. When Richard arrives, Gaunt frankly spells out how Richard has mismanaged affairs:

> Thy death-bed is no lesser than thy land
> Wherein thou liest in reputation sick (2.1.95ff).

England has become Richard's deathbed. The cause, according to Gaunt, is very clear: the flatterers who inhabit the court. Richard is sick, but he listens to the wrong physicians: A thousand flatterers sit within thy crown (2.1.100).

Influenced by these flatterers, Richard has sold England for the funds to maintain the luxurious life of the royal household. As happens often in Shakespeare's plays, some of the most incisive commentary is delivered by ordinary folk; in this case it is the gardener who does so. The queen overhears a conversation between the gardener and his servant as he compares the garden with the commonwealth. This comparison, a convention of long-standing, makes it clear that Richard has neglected to pull the hurtful weeds, to cut down the ambitious nobles. Therefore the wild growth flourishes, and the plants and flowers representing the true nobility are passed over. What is more, Richard cynically intends to seize Gaunt's property and threatens him with disaster. Richard's undoing will be caused by his own folly.

Another dark shadow looms over Richard's government; it is the murder of Gloucester. This shadow is introduced early in the play, when in act 1.2 Gloucester's widow urges Gaunt to avenge the death of her husband. Gaunt informs her that it is impossible to carry out her petition, since Richard himself had a hand in her husband's death. And at this point, indeed, the motif of the two tetralogies is introduced. The murder of a king or a king's son will have ominous consequences. This truth will be repeated in the fate of Richard II himself.

Richard, the Anointed King

Richard now encounters resistance. In Act 3, his authority begins to slip away from him. At first he appeals to the divine right of his kingship:

> Not all the water in the rough rude sea
> Can wash the balm off from an anointed king;
> The breath of worldly men cannot depose
> The deputy elected by the Lord (3.2.54ff).

He may encounter strong opposition, but there is hope. Is not the king's name twenty thousand names? (3.2.85).

Richard's appeal to the divine legitimacy of his kingship is not intended to be hypocritical—no more than when Shakespeare criticizes this dogma in the middle of *Richard II*, for example, does he intend to make a case for the republican point of view.

Not for nothing, as has already been pointed out, will the murder that adheres to Richard continue to fester; one does not just murder a king or a king's son. Bishop Carlyle expresses the official point of view:

> ... The figure of God's majesty,
> His captain, steward, deputy elect,
> Anointed, crowned, planted many years (4.1.125ff.)

He predicts that a judgment will be forthcoming when the king will be deposed and that England will be transformed into "the field of Golgotha and dead man's skulls." (4.1.144) This prophecy will be fulfilled, though the resolution will not arrive until Henry VI. Richard is the anointed king, and that is why his fall is so ominous.

The Lost Image

All this is not to say that Richard is an innocent victim. He is, indeed, the king, but his concrete actions do not follow from a living consciousness of that status. The status of anointed was never intended to approve of tyranny. The prerogatives of royalty were God-given privileges to accomplish good and to exercise justice. To be sure, Richard speaks of justice, but only because he is being pushed into a narrow corner by Bolingbroke. Since Richard is not in a legitimate relationship to God, he becomes dependent on the flatterers with which he has surrounded himself for his sense of identity. Since he has put aside the wisdom of *The Mirror for Magistrates*,[13] he has become dependent in great part for his self-aware-

---

13. This work, published in 1559 by Thomas Marsh, with contributions by various authors, describes the lives of highly-placed folk who, setting themselves before a mirror, take a critical look at their lives. It is one of the "speculum" or mirror-books.

ness as king on what he reads in the eyes of his support group. By doing so, he has hazarded the kingdom itself.

All this comes sharply into focus at the moment when he voluntarily offers to abdicate the throne. Now that his authority has been, in fact, dissipated, the formal delegation of power must take place. It is very important for Bolingbroke that Richard does this voluntarily. And he does make this transfer of power voluntarily, but he turns it into a theatrical spectacle. He asks for a mirror in order to view his own face. As he peers into it, he wonders why his image does not reveal more wrinkles: ". . . O flatt'ring glass / Like to my followers in prosperity, / Thou dost beguile me" (4.1.279ff.). That is, the mirror provides a distorted image of him and does not reflect his true condition. He brings to mind his *followers*, who would have been better called *flatterers*. He raises the mirror, which he had always thought gave him a true recollection of himself. His flatterers have now abandoned him. His "social" ego has dissipated. It was an image in deceitful water. What, then, will provide him an accurate insight into himself? Surely not the mirror. It also gives him a flattering image of himself, since his pain is deeper than the mirror believes. He has been gazing into the wrong mirror, and now the mirror is also lying. Understandably, he looks into his face in astonishment and asks himself:

> . . . Was this the face
> That every day under his household roof
> Did keep ten thousand men? Was this the face
> That like the sun did make beholders wink? (4.1.283ff.).

No, it is his normal self. But who, then, is the real Richard? The mirror is silent about that. In desperation, Richard hurls the mirror into pieces. The image of the mirror has a long tradition.[14] It comes into Shakespeare's work with regularity. An interesting example can be found in Sonnet 62, where the I-person fears self-love as he regards himself as possessing unparalleled beauty. The mirror, however, (my glass) presents him the image of an old man. That brings about repentance, and the conclusion: "Self, so self-loving, were iniquity." In the future he will appraise himself in a *thee*, the still young loved person. The mirror has filled a negative function, but for a new self-image he must look elsewhere. Richard verges

---

This one is intended for magistrates who with the help of this mirror could engage in self-examination.

14. Cf. Melchior-Bonnet, *The Mirror: A History*.

on disillusionment; the image of the flatterers does not ring true, but the image in the mirror provides no answer to the question about the "self." If Richard had looked for a judgment about his royal self not in the mirror of his flatterers, but in God's mirror, he would have understood himself differently. According to *Measure for Measure*, man has "a glassy essence" (2.2.120). He is an image bearer of God and can understand himself only in relationship to God. All this holds even more true for a king. Richard has not done this. In the crisis situation to which he returns, he seeks in vain for a reflection of his true self.

It becomes apparent, in the wake of the mirror scene, where Richard needs to go to find his true self. To do so is painful. The mirror is not useful for disclosing this, and for that reason he will now "face the wind." But the direction he chooses is the way of desperation. He will immerse himself further in the "substance of his grief." This "grief swells with silence in the tortur'rd soul" (4.1.298). From today Richard becomes only the embodiment of his anguish. He flees into a state of melancholy and revels in "sad stories of the death of kings" and speaks of "graves, of worms, and epitaphs" (3.2.156, 145). Something of the theatrical is present in Richard's melancholy. Now that he can no longer glory in the court setting and its rituals, he will project his pain into a theatrical scene. There is something not genuine about Richard. It is as if it is only a dramatic exercise. This theme must have interested Shakespeare, for it comes close to the acting profession. Richard functions as a *persona*, but stands "naked" in actual reality. His death, therefore, will not be true drama either. It is more as if earlier an actor from a drama had disappeared than that a king has been murdered. But what, finally, provides man with a genuine contact with reality, so that he becomes an authentic person?

Richard's Role as King and Death as the Director

Later, in prison, Richard will present himself in all sorts of roles: as a king, as a beggar, and again as a king. In place of the image of the mirror, it is now the metaphor of the actor that comes to the fore. He ends his reflections with the words:

> ... But whate'er I be,
> Nor I, nor any man that but man is,
> With nothing shall be pleas'd, till he be eas'd
> With being nothing (5.5.38ff.).

After all the roles have been tested, and after none of them appear to promise any permanence, and peace has not arrived, he will now scarcely achieve peace by becoming "nothing," which probably strikes very close to death itself. Looking back, he sees his kingship itself as only a role, one which can lead only to deeper despondency. It is an untenable situation. He could mean that he himself exists in a huge place and that he can take into himself everything under the sun, but what self-deception that would be! As he had said earlier:

> For within the hollow crown
> That rounds the mortal temples of a king
> Keeps Death his court, and there the antic sits,
> Scoffing his state and grinning at his pomp,
> Allowing him a breath, a little scene,
> To monarchize, be fear'd, and kill with looks,
> Infusing him with self and vain conceit,
> As if this flesh which walls about our life
> Were brass impregnable; and humour'd thus,
> Comes at the last, and with a little pin
> Bores through his castle wall, and farewell king! (3.2.160ff.).

That is, inside the hollow crown of a king, Death is perched, like a jester, laughing at the crown and ridiculing the pomp which attends the king. Death allows him a small role as king, with power and a space for acting (it is only a *little scene* that he gets to play), feeding his *vain conceit* and the illusion of his immortality. Then Death comes, and bores through his flesh—and the king is gone.

Richard has not remembered that it is God who endows his anointed king and assigns him a role to play; that it is God who has endowed him with sound reasoning. But now Richard has come to believe that within the walls of his crown, Death is actually the king. He is highly skeptical of the role he has played in life and realizes that finally the entire play is an illusion, and that as the pin bores through his flesh, the curtain falls. His good-humored puppet show is cleared away, and what remains is the eternal silence of the dead.

Skepticism

His skeptical talk about death now becomes a skeptical examination of the direction of his life. His kingship is becoming unmasked. He has become vulnerable. In that, all human beings are alike. Why should anyone show honor to a king? Why does he deserve the social spectacle, with all the distinctions, decorum, and loyalty pledges?

It is all vanity, an effort to deny one's humanness. Therefore:

> Throw away respect,
> Tradition, form, and ceremonious duty,
> For you have but mistook me all this while.
> I live with bread like you, feel want,
> Taste grief, need friends: subjected thus,
> How can you say to me I am a king? (3.2.172ff.).

Richard perceives a gap between person and royalty. He has lately come to realize that he is a vulnerable individual, that he needs bread like any other, that he experiences deprivation, experiences sorrow, and needs friends. We hear not a word about his sacred anointing and the divine legitimacy which still distinguishes him from others. Richard has felt honored in his role as king, a calling not shaped by other men, but by which he has, through vain spectacles, forfeited his authority by permitting himself to be seduced and influenced by those who surrounded him. A true king carries out his right calling and, what is more, realizes that he is no more than a humble person, as dependent for his creaturely needs as every other person. This insight, he realizes, has come too late. There is no "normal" life possible for a deposed king. We see him now as imagining another life, supposing that he is a pilgrim, and that he can exchange his royal dignity for the habit of a pilgrim:

> I'll give my jewels for a set of beads;
> My gorgeous palace for a hermitage;
> My gay apparel for an almsman's gown'
> My figur'd goblets for a dish of wood;
> My scepter for a palmer's walking staff;
> My subjects for a pair of carved saints (3.3.147ff.).

Naturally, it is an appealing prospect, at the end of his reign, with the continuing threats on his life, to lay aside his crown in this way. His life as a pilgrim resembles a restful oasis, and he will gladly exchange his jewels, palace, robe of state, decorative plate rack, and scepter for a rosary, a hut, a pilgrim mantel, a wooden dish, and stained glass windows. His purpose from now on is, however, a deep longing to remove himself from the world, and he therefore declares once more his penchant for death:

And my large kingdom for a little grave,
A little little grave, an obscure grave (153 ff.).

The other options for his life are not to be taken seriously. The flight to achieve rest is a disguised death wish. The tragedy of Richard is that he remains a stranger to himself.

Richard the Monomaniac King

Richard has not understand himself in the light of an authentic calling. He did not "read" the text which held him in its grip and provided him with an identity. He vacillates here and there with the possibility of regeneration through genuine repentance. Before he reached for the mirror he said:

I'll read enough
When I do see the very book indeed
Where all my sins are writ, and that's myself (4.1.273ff.).

Here he entertains the possibility of a sharp turn, where he can direct his life once more into a viable existence, however modestly. What is required, according to the book of moral responsibility, of ethics, is that he achieve an authentic contact with reality, however painful that process would be, since that would imply compunction and repentance. He finally chooses instead the tearful way, the way of self-pity, and thus the more significant possibilities slip away.

What is of great relevance here is that Henry V, the son of Henry IV, chooses a different way. Before the battle of Agincourt, he stays behind, alone. He reflects on the shameful deed perpetrated against Richard:

Not today, O Lord,
O not today, think not upon the fault
My father made in compassing the crown.
I Richard's body have interred new (*Henry V*, 4.1.289ff.).

It is as if the punishment due to Richard has not yet been exercised, has so far been postponed. It may appear, since we have heard his thoughts, that Richard's life was not without some depth. Indeed he becomes interesting as we witness his unmasking. But upon closer examination we discover that he is as much a monomaniac as before. He becomes animated in his suffering, but that is more a contrived than a genuine sorrow, though it must also be remembered that he has been dismissed and taken captive.

The Suicide of Thought

As Richard sits in prison, the image of Jack of the Clock occurs to him (5.5.60). Time is passing like the hand on a clock, as a whining and weeping clockwork, with only one change possible: it will become idle. We next see him attempting to relate images of his prison to reality. In doing so, however, he creates a world with such contradictions that his efforts afford him no relief. His thoughts dart hither and yon and find no place to which they can attach themselves. They keep breaking off. What is remarkable is that as his thoughts dart here and there, he compares them with "the thoughts of things divine." But neither do these go anywhere. He gives as examples two sayings of Jesus. The first one reads, "Come, little ones," a reference to the passage "Let the children come to me" (Matt. 19:22–24.) The second one reads, "It is as possible to enter the kingdom as it is for a camel to go through the eye of a needle." These two passages, in the context of grace and judgment, hardly present themselves as relevant to the ebb and flow of his thoughts. They reflect his contradictory state of mind—really, the death of his thoughts. They do not open themselves up to a level where they can serve as a liberating paradox.

But these very thoughts could provide an opening to Richard's soul. A fallen king, deprived of his dignity, and now an ordinary person, he could come to understand whom a king is expected to serve. He would need, at the same time, to understand that only confession and repentance, releasing and handing over the gateway to the kingdom, will suffice in his situation. But now he lets his thoughts clash and strike against each other. In the prison of his mind, all the words from Scripture serve little purpose; they are no more than images and can no longer provide any healing. From the depths of his despair, the "thoughts of things divine" die a quiet death. Richard is painfully captured by his illusory world; he is too much of an actor for the words of Scripture to enable him to get his proper bearings.

It is as if the European spirit has become detached from the heavens—whose book of life read just by itself becomes merely a compilation of contradictions and fragments. Meanwhile, while he is in prison, he does make some progress in his situation. Richard's royal presence in its decline is impressive. Still, his death is near, as a flickering candle, also as he lets out a "mount, mount, my soul! thy seat is up on high" (5.5.111). Richard certainly elicits sympathy from the public. He is a living figure, open to the world, very different from Richard III, who is locked up in himself. This openness comes to its fullest expression in his relationship with his wife. Here we get talk of genuine love. His presence is here at its best. His wife, however, must go into exile and Richard, alone, to "the north / where shivering cold and sickness pines the clime" (5.5.76).

Richard, A Second Fall

The fall of Richard, as has been said previously, does not stand by itself. To be sure, he is merely a king, but his downfall gives us pause. In the scene previously referred to, in which the queen, Richard's wife, over-hears a conversation between the gardener and his servant, she hears talk about the dethroning of Richard. When she hears this, she leaps out and reproaches the gardener for talking about "a second fall of cursed man" (3.4.76). The *downfall* (3.4.79) of Richard is here referred to as "a second fall of cursed man."[15] In that way this fall is a mirror image of the first fall. That furnishes food for thought. The uncertain person, in denial of his status as God's image bearer, will have an identity problem. How must these words be interpreted? Does not such a person oscillate between pride, vanity, and the death wish? What is there to which one can fasten himself? His social ego is fragile—most certainly when it is not sustained by a higher loyalty. The comment which follows is pregnant with meaning:

> Alack the heavy day,
> That I have worn so many winters out,
> And know not now what name to call myself! (4.1.257ff.).

He has been deprived of all his titles and no longer knows what name he should give himself. He is searching for a new title, a new identity, a new mirror in which he can recognize himself once more. *The mirror of glass* provides an image of what is actually the case. Hamlet is called *the glass of fashion* (3.1.147) so that anyone who looks into it may learn how

15. Cf. the rebellion of Scrooge, the Archbishop, against the lawful authority of King Henry V, which the latter called "another fall of man" (*Henry V*, 2.2.142).

he must conduct himself. What becomes obvious is that the theatrical self also functions as a mirror. Hamlet puts into words the meaning as it applies to the stage, "to hold as 't were the mirror up to nature" (3.2.18).[16]

Which mirror is it that can provide an image of life in which mankind can recognize himself? Is there a mirror which will inform him of his status without his urge to break off from what he sees? Is there such a thing as a *speculum humanae salvationis*?[17] Richard has no answer for that question either. Does the knowledge of the "I" lie in the direction of increasing one's mirroring the self? This will be the way which in modern times will be employed with increased frequency. The "I" word in this sense always means more than a solitary "I." Can self-reflection carried on without a horizon of understanding yield more than a duplicate of his own solitary self?

The problem of *Richard II* is the loss of the image of the king. In Richard the metaphysical luster that attaches to royalty has been extinguished. And although this luster has not been entirely dampened (neither has it been for Shakespeare), and though the centuries that are to follow may try to see the kingship in that original light, the preceding events will serve to extinguish the sacramental sense and substitute for it a secular revolution. When this takes place, that mediating image of kingship which functioned for the common man as he faced the question of human identity, will be lost.

How is man now to understand himself? What mediating agency stands between solitary man and his transcendental destiny? Except for the image of the king, all other images have been rejected. Man is the microcosm who understands himself in the light of the macrocosm. Although the Renaissance had cherished these representations, it had also put the axe to them.

These mediating images in Christian Europe were assigned, for the most part, a secondary status. Some folk, who regarded themselves in terms of the microcosm and macrocosm formula, foresaw the warning signs. However, up to this point these representations had been regarded as valid; they were seen as constructs to be understood as direct

16. This statement is a tribute of Samuel Johnson to Shakespeare, when he describes the playwright's work as "the mirror of life." This mirror provides not only a favorable account, but also has the function "to instruct by pleasing."

17. This is the title of a medieval compilation of representations of scenes out of the gospels and saints' lives.

derivations from nature in the light of the transcendental. Human nature is not self-explanatory but points to one beyond himself and requires one above to endow it with an identity. This assertion is also under stress in modern times. Human nature is seen as a self-authenticating whole, sufficiently capable of understanding oneself.

It is a fact that the Reformation provided an answer to the loss of these traditional representations. Its answer was itself a form of iconoclasm insofar as these images were seen not as deriving from an original human nature positioned near God, but as having been locked out from that nature. This iconoclasm was intended to place man under an open heaven once again. It can, however, very readily shoot beyond that target. The result is that man comes to stand alone in a hostile cosmos and with a thoroughly secular history. All this leads ultimately to a drama of solitary man, drama for which much evidence exists in our theaters.

Shakespeare's *Richard II* throws the question of man's identity into bold relief. What name is appropriate for man to define himself? In the Christian tradition that question is answered with a reference to the original image of man, namely, that of Son of Man.

The Suffering King

In the wake of the preceding discussion, I ask permission to provide a last word in order to elucidate a matter which until now has remained in the shadows. I have emphasized strongly Richard's subjective attitude that came to the fore most obviously at the moment when he surrendered his crown. Depression and a longing for death come to expression. For all that, it remains clear that Richard's fall is one permeated with tragic dimensions. His fall creates a vacuum. He is not a scoundrel, but an anointed king. He has not acquired the crown through murder or guile but was legally crowned as the legitimate successor of King Edward III, according to the law of nations. And although he sometimes played the role of a tyrant and committed administrative faults (especially yielding to the powerful influence of a select group of "chosen ones"), it cannot be said that he became a criminal. His fall, therefore, must be seen objectively as the fall of an anointed king. The Bishop of Carlisle sets forth very clearly the ominous implications of this catastrophe:

> And shall the figure of God's majesty,

> His captain, steward, deputy elect,
> Anointed, crowned, planted many years,
> Be judg'd by subject and inferior breath,
> And he himself not present? O forfend it, God,
> That in a Christian climate souls refin'd
> Should show so heinous, black, obscene a deed! (4.1.125ff.).

The bishop here speaks clearly about the deposition of a legitimate king, the manifestation of God's majesty. And although the deposition of Richard appears to be an internal necessity, a measure of guilt attaches to his actions which will be operative to the third generation.

In the person of Richard as legal king who becomes dethroned, imprisoned, and finally murdered, the figure of Christ shines through. Richard himself has understood his sufferings in this light. As Richard arrives to deliver up his crown and sees the people applaud him, he laments:

> . . . Yet I will remember
> The favours of these men. Were they not mine?
> Did they not sometime cry "All hail" to me?
> So Judas did to Christ (167ff.).

And even later, as other spectators appear who themselves will undo his royal trappings, he adds:

> Though some of you, with Pilate, wash your hands,
> Showing an outward pity—yet you Pilates
> Have here deliver'd me to my sour cross,
> And water cannot wash away your sin (239ff.).

The death of Richard will bring up a Golgotha, a field of dead man's skulls (4.1.144). It is noteworthy that Richard sees himself as mirroring the fate of Christ. This identification is not arbitrary. Richard is seen objectively as the anointed king, and his deposition is an act of sacrilege. He has been betrayed by his friends. He is deposed in a process that has a show of legitimacy but which actually camouflages a great injustice. And he is finally murdered. It is by no means a resort to fantasy, a lapse into megalomania or false pathos whenever Richard draws these comparisons. In a Christian culture Christ is preeminently the suffering figure, the matrix through which one's own existence is clarified. This surely holds true for a king. It is precisely because of such identification that Richard's abdication evokes a chilling shudder.

Although Richard has failed as a king, and although in reaction to his deposition he mouths some empty words, one ought not deny that there is a greatness in his fall, that he is greater in his fall than he was in life. Now, standing in the shadow of the suffering Christ, he regains his dignity and eloquence. He becomes "a king in woe" (3.4.97). To the spectators, the death of this suffering king, mirroring as it does the fate of Christ, is of more worth than a mere political murder. "Under the skin," the image of Richard merges with that of Christ. His figure, therefore, bears a greater impact than a merely political event carries. The mourning at the end of the play is a mourning of metaphysical proportions. Henry Bolingbroke himself will don black mourning garments and makes a pledge to go on pilgrimage to the Holy Land "to wash this blood off from my guilty hand" (5.5.50). The reverberations of these events are religious ones. Richard is a post-representation of Christ, and his death leaves an impression long after the penitential prayers and pilgrimages.

3

Measure for Measure

Measure for Measure is a play that is ordinarily classified with the group called *problem plays*. Other plays which belong in this category are *Troilus and Cressida* and *All's Well that Ends Well*.[1] The last named especially exhibits many similarities to *Measure for Measure*. They are called problem plays because a very specific problem or dilemma lies at the heart of the play, a dilemma that requires illumination from diverse angles. Moreover, these plays do not fit well under any of the other categories (comedies, tragedies, history plays, and tragic-comedies).

The title, *Measure for Measure*, already suggests that it needs attention from a theological point of view. It points to Matthew 7:2, "With what measure you measure, it shall be measured to you again." The measure which the main character of the play, Angelo, imposes on another, will turn out to be the very measure by which he himself will be judged. The central problem can also be described as a relationship between justice and judicial proficiency on the one hand, and grace (mercy) on the other hand. Through a masterful interweaving of the text, Shakespeare approaches the central theme from many angles.

Although *Measure for Measure* is based on a Christian worldview, it is inaccurate for one to view it as a Christian allegory. In that case, the duke gets to be seen as a personification of God, and Isabella, representing humanity, as the chosen bride of Christ. The plays of Shakespeare do not propose outlines of ethical or dogmatic theses; this observation applies to *Measure for Measure* as well. They are secular plays, and the meanings are implied in the actions of the play themselves. As already stated, this does not exclude a "spiritual" interpretation. On the contrary, it is in the very

---

1. See also Tillyard, *Shakespeare's Problem Plays*.

management of the action that the important spiritual dimensions come into focus—issues which have everything to do with a Christian reading of life and thought.

The Narrative

Measure for Measure is set in Vienna, whose duke has ruled for many years but who, at the opening, has resolved to temporarily resign his office. He pretends that he will be moving to one or another dukedom, but, in reality, he remains in Vienna, clothed as a monk, and thus becomes a spectator of life in his own state. He transfers his authority to a surrogate, Angelo. The reason for his dramatic move is this: that he wishes to reinstate and instill reverence for the laws that he has let languish. He judges that Angelo is suitably equipped for his new role. At the same time, he is not without doubts about Angelo. Still, Angelo has always been regarded as an outstanding, highly moral, highly-principled person, but will he also sustain this moral excellence when he becomes ruler over the state? In one way or another, Angelo has goaded the duke, and assigning his authority to Angelo is the duke's way of putting Angelo to the test.

Once Angelo becomes the governor, he immediately makes his presence felt. He arrests anyone who has transgressed the laws pertaining to sexual morality and sentences that person to death—among them, Claudio, the character about whom much of the play revolves. He has gotten Juliet pregnant; though the couple were already betrothed they were not yet legally married.[2] Claudio is guilty according to the letter of the law, but, at the same time, one suspects that Angelo had already anticipated arresting Claudio as one of his goals. After a series of unsuccessful efforts to bring about a change of heart in Angelo, Claudio's sister, Isabella, is enlisted as a last resort to plead his cause. Isabella is a devout woman, at the point of becoming a nun. She is persuaded to plead for her brother through a friend of Claudio, (a person of a doubtful reputation, named Lucio). Isabella does proceed to plead for Claudio's freedom. At first Angelo will not hear of the possibility, but in a sudden change of mind he

---

2. This matter concerns the so-called *sponsalia per verba de praesenti*. It was a declaration, confirmed by oaths, to enter into marriage, although the actual wedding ceremony for one reason or another was still future. Later the play mentions a *sponsalia per verba de futuro*. In that case the marriage is still dependent on a number of conditions to be met, usually connected with the bride's dowry.

reconsiders. He proposes that he will free Claudio on the condition that she agree to spend a night with him in bed.

The duke now faces some intricate complications. He has also heard that Isabella has firmly refused Angelo's overtures and that she has also candidly informed her brother about her intentions. Finally, the duke invents a ruse. Isabella would seem to accede to Angelo's bargain, but it will actually be a certain Mariana on whom he will satisfy his lust. This Mariana had earlier been engaged to Angelo, but for some minor cause he had broken the engagement.[3] Without his knowledge, Angelo shares his bed with Mariana. The following day, however, he still orders Claudio to be beheaded. Through the duke's behind the scenes intervention, a way out is found—the head of someone who, through a series of circumstances, has died, now gets delivered to Angelo. Ultimately, the duke returns and establishes justice; the facts of all the ins and outs of the case come to light. Angelo himself has now become subject to the death penalty, but Isabella pleads for his life. Claudio marries Juliet in good order. And the duke, who himself has now been smitten with love, proposes marriage to Isabella.

Tolerance or Punishment

Measure for Measure plays out in Vienna. For well-informed people, however, it was obvious that Vienna conjured up for Shakespeare the contours of London. In this roundabout way, Vienna could serve to bring before the London public moral ambiguities similar to those existing in Vienna.

An important problem in *Measure for Measure* concerns the question of how the laws were to be applied in the community and, particularly, how the sanctions against infractions of the law were to be treated. The duke himself has permitted too much leniency. After fourteen years he has come to realize that this indifference has led to an unsustainable situation:

> . . . in time the rod
> Becomes more mock'd than fear'd: so our decrees,
> Dead to infliction, to themselves are dead,
> And Liberty plucks Justice by the nose,
> The baby beats the nurse, and quite athwart
> Goes all decorum (1.3.26ff.).[4]

---

3. This involves, again, the *sponsalia per verba de futoro*. See previous note.

4. The author provides a Dutch translation of this passage. I will indicate future instances of this practice by the phrase "Dutch translation."

That is, whenever a police agent can no longer enforce the law, he becomes a laughing stock. Freedom becomes liberty to do whatever one pleases, and such a situation adversely affects the very structure of the community. The consequences of a culture of tolerance are ominous. It may be that people, even high-principled people, agree to overlook these transgressions by appealing to the virtue of charity, or by insisting that they themselves do not break these laws, but over a long period of time the fruits of such indifference become very bitter and sour. The danger of such attitudes of a culture of lenience is the supposition of an optimistic view of man's nature, namely, that by maintaining an attitude of tolerance, a community will maintain enough respect for the laws to insure a cohesive society. This is an illusion. Whenever mankind refuses to submit to the yoke of law, the spirit of lawlessness, which always lies dormant, will inevitably make itself felt. The duke understands well that the time has come for a change in direction. However, after such a long period of practicing tolerance has been in play, he must establish legitimacy for such a change:

> Sith 'twas my fault to give the people scope,
> 'Twould be my tyranny to strike and gall them
> For what I bid them do: for we bid this be done,
> When evil deeds have their permissive pass,
> And not the punishment (1.3.35ff.).[5]

That is, the judge, or government official who tolerates evil actually stimulates it. The implicit message of toleration is this: Tread easily on us. Therefore, the one who promotes tolerance becomes an accessory to lawlessness and actually stimulates it. The duke, however, is well aware of the arbitrariness and tyranny that can follow in the wake of abrupt changes. He holds himself accountable for the existing chaos. In a democratic society the only way for him to proceed is to resign. The duke does not consider that but instead tentatively intends to return in order to provide another person the possibility of introducing a stricter way of life.

So far, so good. But strict governance creates its own problems. The duke's substitute, Angelo, will be guided by the letter of the law—and he relishes the opportunity to do so. By coincidence, Claudio becomes the first victim. The penalty for sexual immorality is death. This, by the way, is a practice never carried out in all of Europe. Shakespeare has deliberately

---

5. Dutch translation.

contrived a situation that will permit him to set up the problem as sharply as possible. But he does not choose this example altogether out of thin air, either, for in London, too, sound laws existed about morality and decency that authorities were obliged to enforce. What must one think, for example, about the brothels? In *Measure for Measure* it appears that brothels and the pimps associated with them played a prominent role in the city's life. These were prosperous enterprises. The city of Vienna (London) teems with illegal sexual traffic. As the duke, clothed as a friar, himself puts it later:

> Here in Vienna,
> Where I have seen corruption boil and bubble
> Till it o'errun the stew (5.1.315ff.)

However enlightened a society may be, the necessity for lines to be drawn is always present. These limits may be somewhat fluid, but it is an irrefutable given that they must then be monitored. This pertains also to sexual morality. In our common life together we impose penalties for incest, sex with minors, and sexual intimidation and ravishment.

Angelo undoubtedly was of a mind that action was needed, and by accident Claudio becomes the first victim. Angelo justifies his conduct in his dealings with his co-directors, Escalus and, later, to Isabella, with a reference to the duke himself: he who only threatens and never strikes makes a useless scarecrow of the law, a spot for perching instead of taking flight. He is above all convinced that a judge should serve as an impersonal mouthpiece for the law as written. He does not speak as a person (though at the very first, and only then, as he needs to examine himself preparatory either to examine or condemn another), but as judge. That, then, becomes his exact responsibility.

A marginal note is in order here. Naturally, the law must be enforced, but a true, worthy judge does more than mechanically apply the written rules. Strict justice without wisdom and without the ability to interpret the law leads to inhumane rigidity. Human nature cannot thrive without the law, but he who supposes he needs only to apply the law to the case does not represent judicial acumen. *Summus ius* becomes *summa iniuria*. Or, to cite from the *Basilicon Doron* of James I: "Lawes are ordained as rules of virtuous and social living, and not to be snares to trap your good subjects: and therefore the lawe must be interpreted acoording to the meaning, and not the literal sense . . . And as I said of Uiustice, so say I of Clemencie . . . *Nam in medio stat virtus*."[6]

The wise governor will incline towards moderation. A rigid application of the law can lead to injustice and hypocrisy. The human factor, even in the public domain, cannot be ruled out. Everywhere and always the law has to do with people, and it is a bad omen whenever the officer, magistrate, or judge becomes a thoughtless official whose interpretation does not go beyond the literal wording of the law. A society without a human face becomes just as inhumane as a society without law.

Another point to consider is this: that too great a significance can be given to law. According to Angelo, a strict interpretation of the law will exert a beneficial influence and will thereby insure that sins "have no successive degrees" (2.2.99). With this he overestimates the significance of the law, or underestimates the subtlety and seriousness of the infraction. Angelo also proceeds with an optimistic view of human nature. The law does not, to be sure, improve mankind, but at best will exert a restraining function. Angelo lets himself believe the idle hope that laws and a society of people will generate a good world. That is to suppose that if one can start with the law and well-disposed people, then people on their own will begin to be good and regulate themselves by the law. He will come to learn in a painful way how unfounded such a picture turns out to be.

Justice and Grace

Now we come to an issue of great importance for *Measure for Measure*. Justice does not relate only to restraint but also to grace. It is Isabella who initiates the argument for grace. Whenever Angelo asserts his authority by underscoring the clear statement of the law and makes it clear that Claudio, according to the law, is guilty, Isabella plays her strongest trump card. She says, in one of the most beautiful passages:

> . . . Alas, alas!
> Why, all the souls that were, were forfeit once,
> And He that might the vantage best have took
> Found out the remedy. How would you be
> If He, which is the top of judgment, should
> But judge you as you are? O, think on that,

6. Cited in "Introduction" to Lever, *Measure for Measure*, xlix.

And mercy then will breathe within your lips,
Like man new made (2.2.72ff.)[7]

Isabella here refers to divine justice. The judge himself is subject to the highest judge. Along with that we rightly stand before him as guilty persons, clearly disqualified by the law. But God has found a way to rescue man from the punishment due him, even though it might be to his advantage to demand, and in full, all the requirements of justice. Shakespeare here points to the way of redemption through Jesus Christ, an initiative of God's grace, which, without violating justice, can still free man from the curse of sin. This divine formula for justice must now make its way into earthly jurisprudence. Since God has been creative in finding a remedy, man needs to do the same from now on. The image of grace that breathes through the lips is an allusion. God created Adam at one time by blowing breath into his nostrils. Adam, however, fell into sin. Thereupon God breathes on him anew through the spirit of grace in an act of re-creation. Through this, man obtains the gift of the spirit. Man himself will now also breathe out the spirit of grace. God has, thus, not only provided a way of escape, but has renewed man as well.

This is a beautiful exposition of the gospel. The question, however, is whether this teaching is appropriate in the context of the human administration of justice. Can the gospel serve as a guide for structuring a society? Upon further reflection, it becomes apparent that Isabella's argument is both too rigid and too simple. It turns the state into a church and earthly jurisprudence into a heavenly one—or, at least, an ecclesiastical one. The Christian can forgive the murderer of his beloved, but the judge is obliged to punish him. More than that, it is possible for grace to become a device by which judicial authority can be manipulated. Whenever Mistress Overdone, a brothel keeper, cries out for mercy, Escalus remarks, "This would make mercy swear and play the tyrant" (3.2.188).[8] The duke himself notes that mercy can become a pretext for vice: "When vice makes mercy, mercy's so extended / that for the fault's love is th' offender friended" (4.2.110).[9] Grace then becomes a cheap commodity. As Heinrich Heine says—forgiveness is God's job—then an arbitrary plea for mercy becomes a false plea, and the same will happen in the administration of justice.

7. Dutch translation.
8. Dutch translation.
9. Dutch translation.

Isabella's plea for mercy, though, differs from one seeking an excuse. It could be that the watershed between the "kingdom of God" and "the kingdom of this world" has in a strict sense, vanished. It is all about finding a *remedy*, and that is something different from the way justice is commonly shoved off to the side. Moreover, God himself has exercised grace without shoving justice off to the side. The ransom has been paid by the Son himself. A facile secularization of grace will, in practice, lead to a cheap tolerance that, eventually, raises the problem once more of a society degenerating into chaos. How can man permit the exercise of grace without diminishing the role of authority? We must pay careful attention now, for we are entering territory for which some sensitivity, some "precision tuning," is crucial.

Another argument which Isabella introduces is one which emerges from an earlier citation, the subject of self-knowledge. Once a person attains a certain prominence, he can hardly be restrained, and fits the following description:

> But man, proud man,
> Dress'd in a little brief authority,
> Most ignorant of what he's most assured
> —His glassy essence—like an angry ape
> plays such fantastic tricks before high heaven
> As makes the angels weep (2.2.118ff.).[10]

These lines are also a gem; they embody deep truth. Man is clothed with temporary authority and pretends, as *proud man*, that he is himself the source from which his authority flows. He is an angry ape. The ape here stands for a vain animal who imitates life and thinks he embodies the real. The earthly judge imitates the authority of the heavenly judge and becomes a laughing stock. Man is an image; he has "a glassy essence," and is not himself an original. It is God who is the original.

All this is a pleasant argument, but it ultimately undermines any form of authority. It is a truth that can also be used—unintentionally—as grist in the mill of every scoundrel. In the name of modesty and under the guise of the humble idea that no one possesses authority innately, all earthly authority can be undermined. But precisely because man is an image bearer of God, he can serve as a judge in appropriate situations. He or she then becomes obliged to reflect God's justice upon the earth.

10. Dutch translation.

Thus, he can properly become a true judge. Perhaps this is what Isabella means when she contends that a judge receives his authority on loan. That authority is genuine authority, but one must make himself accountable. Such a judge must not be overly rigid, for if he is, he will be seen to suppose that he is a perfect embodiment of the right. How can both of these motives be affirmed?

The Person of the Rector

Measure for Measure now takes a turn in which the person of the judge will be the center of discussion. We will also attempt a keen analysis of how, in the apotheosis of the play, heavenly jurisprudence sheds a bright light on what happens in judicial proceedings on the earth.

Angelo takes refuge behind the law. This is good, since we now have an objective state of law and order, of which the middle class government is the embodiment and without its being twisted to one's personal advantage. However, the objective and the subjective cannot be that easily separated. Naturally, Angelo has it right when he claims that when the law speaks, no discussion is allowed. "It is the law, not I, condemn your brother" (2.2.80). Still, the question remains whether the administration of justice may be of as impersonal a character as Angelo claims. In either case, we confront the question of what happens when the judge as a private person does not hold himself accountable to the norm that he prescribes for others. That leads to cynicism. There arises a tension between a strong rigid interpretation of the law, without reference to human feelings, and a lax personal morality that, with all its talk, glosses over the infraction.

Angelo approaches Claudio's case without any human emotion. He is totally devoid of pity, an attitude which leads to Escalus's lament, "If my brother wrought by my pity, it should not be so with him" (3.2.204).[11] Thus, the play acquires a deeper meaning, one to which the title itself points: "With what measure you measure, you shall yourself be measured" (Matt 7:2). Or, in the words of Paul (Rom 2:22), "You say, 'Do not commit adultery'; but are you an adulterer?" This question is put not only to the management of a civil state. It applies also to the person of the judge. Who are you, really? Much of the drama of *Measure for Measure* hinges very directly on the person of the judge.

11. Dutch translation.

Now a second motive comes to light. The duke, it seems, has left the city not only to instill new life into the authority of the law. He wishes also to test his surrogate, Angelo. He is reputed to be a virtuous man, "scarce confesses / that his blood flows; or that his appetite / is more to bread than stone" (1.3.51vv). The duke will be watching what happens whenever such a one is genuinely tested. So long as you are securely removed from the turbulence of life, you will find it easy to be a shining white knight. But how do you fare in the heat of the strife? That is the question. In fact, the duke contrives by means of his departure precisely to establish a context in which he can put a man's virtue to the test before his very own eyes. The question of whether such a strategy is acceptable lies outside the bounds of the drama. It must be remembered that Angelo is not coerced to fail the test. He can remain upright. His personal integrity is on the line. Angelo is being given the chance to display it. Men must embark this one time to meet the challenge in actual life. There is a positive reason for doing so:

> Heaven doth with us as we with torches do,
> Not light them for themselves; for if our virtues
> Did not go forth of us, 'twere all alike
> As if we had them not. Spirits are not finely touch'd
> But to fine issues (1.1.32ff.).[12]

Virtue, that is, exists to be exercised. Virtue that lives as "een boekje in een hoekje" (a book in a corner) is hardly a prototype of true virtue. That is a law that applies to Angelo. It is also a law that applies to Isabella. She stands at the point of entering a convent, but now she is being called upon to prove her virtue in the tumult of the world. It is hardly the apex of virtue for her to ask, upon entering the cloister, whether the rules could not be made more stringent (1.4.4).

Angelo is also being challenged to prove himself. He has been placed in a prominent position, but he is now about to experience how dangerous it is for a person to boast about his own rectitude. Angelo thus falls. The temptation to go astray comes from an unexpected source. He succumbs to the power of Isabella's charm, and his passions are aroused. An amorous disposition is not a sin, but as he has not allowed personal feelings of sympathy, his sexual desires gain the upper hand. What is crucial is that, in order to satisfy these sexual urges, he abuses his authority as judge. He will bribe Isabella in order to carry out his sinful passions.

12. Dutch translation.

Shakespeare displays with powerful insight how Angelo's lust has pinned himself into a corner:

> . . . it is I
> That, lying by the violet in the sun,
> Do as the carrion does, not as the flower,
> Corrupt with virtuous season (2.2.165ff.)

That is, while basking in the sun of Isabella's virtuous life, he is hardly a flower that does what flowers do: bloom and emit fragrant scents; he is, instead, like a nasty vulture that is beginning to decompose. "O fie, fie, fie! What dost thou, or what art thou, Angelo?" (2.2.172). This is the moment where Angelo realizes he is being tempted by "the cunning enemy," the devil himself. He is managing to trap Angelo through a virtuous woman: "to catch a saint, / with saints dost bait thy hook" (2.2.180). That he here invokes a saint contradicts the reputation he has established until now, but it also displays his lack of self-knowledge. Here he learns that a world of lust lurks in him as well. It is a world against which not even his prayers can avail. He does move to pray, much as it occurs in *Hamlet* through Claudius, and without results:

> When I would pray and think, I think and pray
> To several subjects: Heaven hath my empty words,
> Whilst my invention, hearing not my tongue,
> Anchors on Isabel; Heaven in my mouth,
> As if I did but only chew his name,
> And in my heart the strong and swelling evil
> Of my conception (2.4.1ff.)[13]

The heavens pale at the power of suggestion from the beautiful Isabella. Here one can ask himself whether a person can escape this dance—whether he can leap away from such a temptation. "The strong and swelling evil / of my conception" is so great that his prayer loses its power (2.4.15). Praying does not help. The law which beats in the veins wins out over the other law. It is important to note, however, that we are not encountering a conflict between fleshly desires and the spiritual life. Angelo turns out to be an admirer of his own rectitude and learns that he is not able to maintain that stand. The reason his prayer fails is not that he has sexual desires but that he turns out to have been a worshiper of

13. Dutch translation.

himself. True piety does not deny one's humanity. Angelo has done just that and now shows that he is not a god, but a man.

Angelo falls, and his fall is great. The satisfaction of his repressed sexual desires that he now undertakes is wicked. He places Isabella in a moral dilemma, springing from his lusts. In a heart that appears as white as snow, there lurks a pool of darkness. As Isabella says,

> ... This outward-sainted deputy,
> ... is yet a devil:
> His filth within being cast, he would appear
> A pond as deep as hell (3.1.88, 91ff.)[14]

The sudden impulse that has led to this reversal exposes the depths of his evil heart—exposing it as a pool deep and dark, like hell. Angelo now falls a second time—by not carrying through with his agreement to free Isabella's brother, but to have him beheaded after all. His motif is fear. He fears that Claudio, once he is freed, will seek revenge (4.5.26ff.) because his freedom has been bought off in such a base manner. His possession still of Isabella, and allowing Claudio to be beheaded, are subordinate to his moral guilt. He falls a third time when he flatly denies the accusations brought against him and, hardhearted as nails in his denial, lets Isabella and Mariana be imprisoned for slandering lawful authority.

What is really at stake is a man who wishes to promote himself. The virtuous person who trumpets his own virtue lacks a measure of self-knowledge, a deficiency that cries to high heaven. "What art thou, Angelo?" A fallen man. It is too simple to regard Angelo as a oafish scoundrel. He is a mirror, and for the very people whom he is obliged to represent. He denies his sexual urges and is thus confronted with his violent nature. He lives without any understanding of pity and mercy. He has no understanding of God, who is not only a stern lawgiver but, above all, a God of grace, *who found out the remedy.* Angelo stands as a stranger respecting this deliverance, and now becomes the ape of God, an *angry ape* who discovers a *foul redemption* (2.4.113). Ultimately, however, a way will open up for him, and that is because he will be shown mercy. The person who banishes grace from his life will take a fall and will then become dependent on mercy from another. In this case, it will be from Isabella, who will propose an amazing way to achieve Angelo's liberation.

---

14. Dutch translation.

The Nun from the Religious House

And what about Isabella? She has elicited very diverse reactions from all sorts of spectators and readers. Some see her as a moral freak. "Her virtue is monstrously rigid and her chastity a bit too much of a veneer."[15] Isabella herself has been spared from such uncharitable judgments. Isabella is too complex a character to describe without our acknowledging the ambiguities. Perhaps Isabella has too little insight into her own nature. She possesses more feminine charms than she is aware of. But they do, in fact, work their power, however unobtrusively. Unobtrusively? Surely not altogether so. She reacts as if she were allergic to sexuality, describing it as a *vice that most I do abhor* (2.2.29). One becomes suspicious, however, when she describes sex before marriage as the worst of the deadly sins.[16] That verdict is not consistent with the traditional Christian ethic where, rather, pride and envy were ranked as the most serious of the seven cardinal sins. Is she suppressing her sexuality in such talk?

Isabella is now on the spot, having been put there by Angelo. She will bring herself to go to bed with him in order to free her brother. For this, he uses arguments that sound much the same as those that Isabella had used. It is apparent, however, that these two situations have totally different backgrounds:

> Ignominy in ransom and free pardon
> Are of two houses (2.4.111ff.).

In this, Isabella's argument is identical. Ransom through shame and the free word of forgiveness can have a plausible similarity in their forms, but they are, in fact, poles apart. Not everything has been said, of course. However, Angelo proposes a devil's dilemma to her; Isabella must consult her attitudes as she evaluates her own integrity. How will she play the game? Must she go along with Angelo's proposal and thereby rescue her brother? Must she out of love for her brother submit to this degradation of herself? Her goal is worthy; she does wish to have her brother released and has had a lively debate with Angelo about that. Must she concede to Angelo's cunning negotiations and perform what cannot be described otherwise than a sinful act? Or must she reject this deed, since God has

15. Birrell, *Engelse Letterkunde*, 59.

16. In *Macbeth*, Macduff speaks about greed that has tougher roots than "summer-seeming lust."

strictly forbidden, by law, the act of prostitution, in the wake of which she could only let her brother's fate rest with God? In other words, must she exercise obedience with an indifference to the consequences?

A moral choice, however, according to Christian discernment, involves not only the choice being discussed, but also the motivation. And right here is where the problem comes to light. Isabella shrinks before the deed because of the ensuing disgrace. Now she seeks moral support from her brother and pleads with him to have regard for her honor. In a subtle way she permits her encounter with her brother to hinge on the question of her honor. In her first soliloquy she formulates her moral dilemma as follows:

> Then, Isabel live chaste, and brother die;
> More than our brother is our chastity (2.4.183ff.).

Her chastity is more valuable than her brother's life. In the sequel, the matter turns on the phrase "yield my virginity" (3.1.97). The devotional literature of Elizabethan times decries this fixation on one's virginity. So says William Tyndale about Lucrecia: "She sought her owne glory in her chastite and not gods," and, "pryde god more abhorreth then the whordome of anye whor."[17] The sin of pride is worse than the whoredom of Mistress Overdone.

She owns up to what she is whenever Claudio breaks down and asks her to rescue him:

> What sin you do to save a brother's life
> Nature dispenses with the deed so far
> That it becomes a virtue (3.1.133ff.).

This is naturally a naïve account of these cases, because the end does not justify all the means. However, Isabella reacts as if stung by a wasp and begins to curse her brother:

> O you beast!
> O faithless coward! O dishonest wretch!
> Wilt thou be made a man out of my vice? (3.1.137ff.).

Though she had tried to bargain with Angelo by moving him to exercise pity, any form of it has now become a stranger to her. She distances herself from Claudio to the extent that she speculates whether her mother

---

17. *The Obedynce of a Chrysten Man*, cited by Lever, *Measure for Measure*, lxxx, lxxxi.

might not have become estranged from her son at the moment of his conception. She draws a line between her bad brother and his good sister. She sees herself as the daughter of an honorable father whereas her brother could be a bastard. The "die, perish!" (3.1.143) is the heartless speech that could have come as well from an Angelo. Here we begin to see Isabella as someone whose virtue turns in on itself. Is it possible that a criticism of the select group who have turned to monasticism is implied here? The truth is that Isabella displays a secret form of *pride*, which prompts her fixation on her honor and its opposite, *shame*. Where the secret sin of Angelo, pride, is pallid (2.4.10), it appears that Isabella's pride is aroused. Her virtue has become a defensive and self-defensive virtue.

Although she had been prepared to plead for her brother, it now appears that she prizes her own reputation more than the life of her brother. Isabella still has some ways to go. She can make progress only when she exchanges her defensive virtue for an active one. How can things proceed better than when this active virtue appears in the warmth of *mercy*? Actually, things will come to the point where grace will temper justice.

The Duke, or Is Morality Possible?

The duke, who has been the spectator so far, begins increasingly to intervene in these affairs. He has grasped certain strings, prompting moves that inhere in his function as *friar*. He has prepared Claudio for his death and has directed that Isabella be offered spiritual assistance. In increasing measure, however, he becomes the director behind the screen. He devises the strategy of finding a substitute for Isabella. He gives orders that Claudio is not to be beheaded. By the end of the fourth act, however, he has completely returned to his role as manager. In the fifth act the true ins and outs of the events will come to light in a most remarkable way. "Much has been written in defense of the second half of *Measure for Measure*, but it is surely a muddle."[18] And a *muddle* is surely the right word. Shakespeare has perhaps permitted the duke to become so heavily involved in order to achieve the impression he wishes to leave. The duke is not completely in charge, however; he is also dependent on the agency of providence. Since no one's head is available to substitute for Claudio's, the pirate Ragozine, who resembles Claudio, is kind enough to die the night

18. Kermode, *Shakespeare's Language*, 164.

before. This proves unmistakably the duke's limitations as a director. He is, however, in his role as spectator from below the horizon, responsible for preventing the play from declining into a tragedy. The criticism that *Measure for Measure* is in fact a tragedy and only artificially preserved as a tragi-comedy is, in my opinion, incorrect. The manner by which the duke averts the tragedy is, indeed, wonderful, but wholly congruent with the situation at the opening of the play. Above all, the mantra of *found out the remedy*, which Isabella acknowledges somewhat mistakenly, does, in fact, ring true. Apart from that, the duke is more than a mere puppeteer who pulls the strings to his marionettes. He prompts Isabella to the first deed as a prelude to an active virtue. More than that, he himself will be surprised at her second act. Her first act is to go along with the bed-trick with the argument: "Virtue is bold, and goodness never fearful" (3.1.208). He tutors the virtue in her so that these work positively rather than negatively. He sees to it above all that her virtue is not altogether spotless. Does she not need to confess to the agreement that passed her lips to capitulate to Angelo's temptation? More than that, she must confront her shame. The duke, therefore, arranges for Isabella to compromise herself in an unacceptable manner. Isabella becomes vindicated about her integrity in view of her careful deliberations (and in that respect the duke is more generous than many critics), but the duke does not see this as an end in itself, since virtue can be so easily compromised. In fact, now Isabella works hand in hand with the deed involving Mariana, whose actions are, naturally, as blameworthy as is the deed of Claudio and Juliet. However, because of Mariana's love and the prior right that she has over Angelo, Isabella consents to the plan. From a pedagogical and moral point of view, this is a master stroke of the duke.

The duke comes with an extreme proposal to Mariana, offering to find *a way out*. This looks very much like a "by chance" occurrence. All of a sudden, there is this Mariana. That is really true. The world does not work without coincidences. Is that not precisely the nature of reality? The moral that the duke proposes does not follow a mere book, but the world in which morality is lived out is even less a formula from a book. Invention and creativity do not come to us with empty hands. Cases like Mariana's will occur and will do so for the not theologically unimportant reason that the providence of God has more to do than to see to it that the trains run on time—though that itself is a marvel. Morality is practiced in an open world. O'Donovan, in his authoritative *Resurrection and Moral*

Order, sets forth this very principle of moral reality.[19] Moral dilemmas can be driven to extremes and considered in the abstract, but God has provided a world hospitable to morality. It is a distortion bordering on a perverse interpretation of the case if we agree to call the play, despite all its violence, a tragedy. Shakespeare has written tragedies also, and they mirror a reality that is all too accurate. However, tragedy is a temporary state of affairs, a departure from the normal order. Tragedy is not by itself the norm. It is even less the ultimate, final chord of history.

Mercy in Action

The apotheosis of the play is indeed amazing but, above all, an impressive work. In the final stages, hearts become revealed and growth has occurred. Isabella plays a dominant role in all this. She cannot be sure whether Claudio is beheaded and cries out to the duke for justice: "Justice! Justice! Justice!" (5.1.26). Where does she stand now with the duke, after all these turns, in the argumentative duel to get someone's ear to listen to her story? She complains to Angelo, with a lament: "I now begin with grief and shame to utter" (5.1.99). She tells about Angelo's deceitful proposal, but follows with this:

> . . . and after much debatement,
> My sisterly remorse confutes mine honour,
> And I did yield to him (5.1.102ff.).

Here Isabella takes an important step. She relegates *sisterly remorse* to a higher priority than honor and chooses sisterly compassion. She had publicly confessed her readiness to distance herself from rescuing her brother, and she is now ready to call her deed a deed of shame. To be sure, she is driven to this to achieve justice against Angelo, but this claim to justice is certainly grounded on the law violated against her brother. Has her cooperation in the bed-trick awakened this growth? In either case, she has developed beyond her former self.

But another step lies in wait for the unmasking of Angelo. The sentence of the duke is clear and seriously intended:

> An Angelo for Claudio, death for death.
> Haste still pays haste, and leisure answers leisure;

19. O'Donovan, *Resurrection and Moral Order*, 120.

Like doth quit like, and Measure still for Measure (5.1.407ff.).[20]

Now Angelo is to be subjected to justice. But an intercessor appears, namely, Mariana, who, despite everything that has befallen her, still wishes to accept Angelo. When her entreaty fails, Isabella comes forward:

> . . . I partly think
> A due sincerity govern'd his deeds
> Till he did look on me (5.1.444ff.)
> . . . His act did not o'ertake his bad intent,
> And must be buried but as an intent
> That perish'd by the way. Thoughts are no subjects;
> intents, but merely thoughts (5.1.449ff.).[21]

Isabella is pleading here for the murderer of her brother. She does this for Angelo mostly out of sympathy for Mariana. Now the gospel principle proves true—the principle that she has tested in the heat of her argumentation. She "finds a way out." Taken by itself, the principle is weak, since Angelo has broken his pledge and has not spared Claudio's life. Later, in good time, it will appear that he who so insisted so strictly on the letter of the law has not committed a sin, but this is accidental and does not settle the matter of his guilt. The deliverance which comes into play is, therefore, not more than an analogy of the divine response. However, as the events turns out, it is indeed an analogy—one which has become flesh and blood through concrete actions. Whoever wishes an improved analogy must not continue to look at matters while stuck in the throes of idealism. Opposed to the jolting deed of Angelo's renunciation of his pledge, there stands the dazzling intercession of Isabella. This intercession on the part of Isabella during the unmasking of Angelo compensates for the man-made solutions in the last scene. And it is very clear that this mercy has not been cheaply bought. Those who offer costly, genuine grace will receive more than a formal bowing of the knee. Those who pour out genuine grace are also authorized to say, "Go, and sin no more." Cheap grace costs nothing from those who offer it; it also benefits the receiver of such grace very little. Costly grace is very different. At its deepest level, therefore, no conflict exists between grace and the law. At a still deeper level, grace and the law are rightly joined, while the law comes into play whenever the light of grace shines upon it.

20. Dutch translation.
21. Dutch translation.

A parallel from recent times is the Truth and Reconciliation Commission, which was established in South Africa after the end of the apartheid administration. Guilt was brought to light and acknowledged; the power of the law then could be applied. What also happened is that the victims forgave the guilty agents. Through these actions of grace, people undertook an effort upon which a society could be established where right and justice could rise above the code of "an eye for an eye and a tooth for a tooth."

Measure for Measure is a study in ethics. G. Wilson Knight states that the poetical force of the play derives from its religious and moral character.[22] He observes that the play does not receive its character from normal life, but from its affinity with a parable. This parable discloses a gospel truth. Knight proves his point by quoting a number of biblical texts which resonate at various points in the play. He points to Matthew 5:12, "And forgive us our debts, as we also have forgiven our debtors." Also, Matthew 10:26, "There is nothing hidden that shall not be revealed." Matthew once again—12:36, ". . . every thoughtless word you speak you will have to account for on the day of judgment." (This applies to the character Lucio, a notorious babbler, whom I have left out in my interpretation.) Matthew 8:9 reads, "Such a great faith have I not seen in all of Israel." (This applies to the prison warder, whom I have also placed outside my treatment.) And there is John 8:11, "Then do I not condemn thee" (the words of Jesus to the woman caught in adultery). They also belong to this group of texts.

I am of one mind with G. Wilson Knight. By that reading, *Measure for Measure* stands out as unique in the works of Shakespeare. It is also the one play in which the very title refers directly to the truths of the gospel.

---

22. Knight, *The Wheel of Fire*, 80.

4

Hamlet

Pandarus: "Sir, I do depend upon the Lord."
Servant: "You are in the state of grace?" 0
Pandarus: "Grace? Not so, friend. "Honour" and "lordship" are my titles."
Troilus and Cressida, 3.1.5, 14ff.

A Somber Work

HAMLET IS WITHOUT A doubt the most enigmatic character Shakespeare
has created. He is an enigma even within the world of the play. Claudius,
Gertrude, Polonius, Rosencrantz, and Guildenstern try in every possible
way to probe his inner life. The public, acquainted with the narrative, does
its own conjecturing, but it is questionable whether their conjectures are
any better. "You that look pale and tremble at this chance, / That are but
mutes or audience to this act, / Had I but time—as this fell sergeant, Death,
/ Is strict in his arrest—oh, I could tell you—But let it be" (5.3.345 ff.). Ultimately the audience does not get to hear what Hamlet wished to say.

And what have the exegetes of the play concluded? Have they been
able to get Hamlet to speak? Or do they agree with what Hamlet himself
says earlier to one of the spies: "There is much music, excellent voice,
in this little organ, yet cannot you make it speak." Playing the flute is a
difficult art, but it is far more difficult to "play" Hamlet. For Hamlet it
is true *par excellence* what, according to Pascal, is true for all mankind:
"Man is an organ, but a strange, whimsical and changeable organ. . . . One
needs to know the location of the keys."[1] I do not pretend either to play
the Hamlet flute or to know where the keys are. Hamlet remains a sphinx,

1. Pascal, *Pensees*, fragment 55 (ed. Laguma).

57

and, in a sense, this is true for the whole play. It is possible that this was one of Shakespeare's intents: an elusive figure set on the stage, who will not entirely yield his hidden secret.

The play *Hamlet* centers on revenge. It stands, thus, in the tradition that Thomas Kyd made popular with his *The Spanish Tragedy*.[2] Shakespeare first attempted this genre in *Titus Andronicus*.[3] *Hamlet* is the mature play, which can be regarded as the climax of the theme. Hamlet learns from a ghost that his father has been murdered. It appears to be ghost of his father himself. Claudius, his brother, is designated as the murderer. Claudius is now king and is married to Gertrude, the wife of his brother, Hamlet senior. Son Hamlet is charged with the mission to avenge the murder. He is willing enough to do so, but situations always arise that give him a reason to procrastinate. The entire play is shaped by the postponement of the ghost's order. In between, a bundle of other things happen. Hamlet, who pretends madness, also has to deal with Ophelia's rejection of his love. This development is brought about by Polonius's forbidding Ophelia to associate with Hamlet. Hamlet moves around mournful and mad, and Claudius and Gertrude, in an attempt to understand him better, engage two old friends from the country for this purpose. They discover even less, and Polonius, who suspects Hamlet's disappointment in love as the cause for his antics, cannot really find the origin of Hamlet's melancholy. In the meantime Hamlet has become increasingly convinced that Claudius has killed his father. He speaks to his mother with high earnestness about her marriage to Claudius, but, without knowing it was he, kills Polonius, who has positioned himself as an eavesdropper behind the screen. Out of concern for revenge by Laertes, son of Polonius, the king has Hamlet sent away, by his "friends" to England. Now Ophelia has become insane and eventually takes her own life. Hamlet never arrives in England because en route he discovers that a plot has been instigated against him that will lead to his death when he arrives there. Through a timely seizure of documents, Hamlet arranges for his escort friends to be killed instead. Hamlet returns, and Laertes returns from abroad in order to avenge his father's death. Claudius cleverly arranges a fencing match

---

2. See McIwraith, ed., *Five Elizabethan Tragedies*. The complete title reads: "The Spanish Tragedie, containing the lamentable end of Don Horatio and Bel-imperia: with the pittifull death of olde Hieronimo." The text dates from 1589.

3. A gruesome play, with scenes that compare with the most shocking scenes in the whole of Shakespeare.

between Hamlet and Laertes. But Laertes uses a poisoned sword. That leads to a dramatic outcome, when all die either from a poisoned sword tip or from a poisoned drink. Hamlet's friend, Horatio, is the only one who can distance himself from this dance of death.

Hamlet is by far the most depressing of all Shakespeare's plays. An important purpose of a tragedy is to bring about in the hearer a catharsis, a purification. Aristotle thought about it in that way.[4] In most of Shakespeare's tragedies we see this come about. But how is it with *Hamlet*? In tragedies one finds a clear link between temptation and a misstep on the part of the lead character and his tragic ending. In all tragedies (if the chief character is not a scoundrel) a strong relationship exists between guilt and penalty. That good people also perish is, true enough, painful to observe, but persons who already die do so because of the righteous ones, such as Cordelia in *King Lear* or Desdemona in *Othello*, and such episodes do arouse pity and fear. In Hamlet that appears less the case. The death of Ophelia is tragic, but she is not an important enough character to arouse in us strong feelings, as we do for Cordelia and Desdemona. The death of Hamlet fits less clearly into the temptation formula of downfall and death. He perishes more or less by accident, as the result of a behind-the-back intrigue. Or does there exist a deeper level of connection among these events?

Helen Gardner speaks somewhere about the "painful, dark, mistrustful world of *Hamlet*." The conclusion of the play is disturbing. The last words of Hamlet resound long after: *The rest is silence*. The stage is strewn with dead bodies, and reports of persons who already died form a buzz around them. All the chief characters perish: Hamlet, Claudius, Gertrude, Ophelia, Polonius, Laertes, Rosencrantz, and Guildenstern. The one person who remains alive and whom Hamlet prevents from committing suicide is Horatio, but he can hardly qualify as a main character. Moreover, he gets assigned the doubtful honor of informing posterity of all the events that have transpired. He will speak "Of carnal, bloody and unnatural acts, / Of accidental judgments, casual slaughters, / Of deaths put on by cunning and forced cause, / And in this upshot, purposes mistook / Fallen on th' inventors' heads" (5.2.360ff.).[5] It is a bloody history, full of violence and misunderstanding that simply sweeps everyone along. Indeed, what is one to make of a play whose action is driven by the ghost

---

4. See Aristotle, *Poetics*, 6; tragedy is divided according to "incidents arousing pity and fear wherewith to accomplish its catharsis of such emotions."

5. Dutch translation of this passage.

of the murdered King Hamlet, the father of Hamlet? Standing among all the dead, the presence of Fortinbras is hardly significant. He will become the new king, but he is not a figure who will generate any sympathy from the spectators. The world of *Hamlet* is well described by one of the guards of the Danish kingdom: "Something is rotten in the state of Denmark" (1.4.90). That element of corruption is what goads on the various characters. Another prominent image in *Hamlet* is that of a festering wound that is covered with a thin gauze and concealed with a veneer of refinement.[6]

In *Hamlet* religious views appear infrequently. To be sure, many references to religion are present, and one cannot understand Hamlet without having a disposition to recognize them. A famous quote (though somewhat ambiguous and often taken out of context) suggests such matters:

> There are more things in heaven and earth, Horatio,
> Than are dreamt of in your philosophy (1.5.166ff.)

Heaven and hell (and purgatory)? These are supposedly opposites. Their role is not an unimportant one in the play. It is impossible to understand Hamlet or Claudius apart from a Christian context. Hamlet himself possesses a religious nature, as will appear in a later analysis, though this disposition appears in a negative form that ultimately kicks off to a positive kernel. From a certain point of view, this anomaly is the really tragic component in this tragedy. This raises a problem not only for the play, but it is also of the utmost importance for the place and significance of Christian belief in the new age.

Although *Hamlet* may leave us with a feeling of depression, it is at the same time also a very lively and compelling play, not least because Hamlet himself is such a fascinating person. Hamlet is someone who expresses himself in a multitude of voices. To be sure, his melancholy is dominant, but he has other moods, such as the hilarious and passionate. Hamlet has a gift for spontaneity and a quick wit. He is sometimes ironical and a master satirist. He speaks always to the point and reacts with animation and presence of mind. Above all, as we can tell from a number of soliloquies, Shakespeare reveals a deep inner life that makes him a truly interesting person. Hamlet is the type of the solitary person who no longer feels at home in his surroundings, though he does not tear himself loose from that environment in an arbitrary manner. In that way

6. Cf. Spurgeon, *Shakespeare's Imagery and What It Tells Us.*

he has emerged as an archetype of European cultural life, alongside Don Quixote, Faust, and Don Juan—types who express fundamental drives of the human spirit and who by so doing become exceptional literary types.

The Morality of Reality: Injustice and Ambiguity

The question regarding the morality of the prevailing society is the central issue in *Hamlet*. To all appearances, all is well in Denmark. King Claudius is a good monarch; he governs the state with wisdom. To be sure, a vacuum exists, some instability, because of the early death of the "old" Hamlet, and though Claudius's opponents (especially Fortinbras) may try to capitalize on the situation, Claudius understands the danger well enough to resist any such opposition. Still, right under the surface something seems amiss at the very heart of this world; some fundamental relationships have been disturbed. In ordinary times, such feelings of unease do not surface readily. People function unconsciously within the existing relationships. The traditional rituals proper to church and society, which offer a sense of transcendence, are in place. But the sudden death of his father, and the fact that his mother "Ere yet the salt of most unrighteous tears / Had left the flushing in her galled eyes" (1.2.154ff.) had married the brother of his father—a man who, according to Hamlet, was by any count inferior to his father—has proved a tremendous shock and has brought about a general feeling of nausea and aversion. Hamlet's mourning for his father is sincere. If that becomes an issue, he makes it clear that it is not a mere ritual, but actual: ". . . but I have that within which passes show" (1.2.85). He upbraids Claudius and his mother Gertrude for the insincerity of their mourning. He asks his mother how authentic her love could be if it could so easily transfer to Claudius. Hamlet is nauseated at such a suggestion, and this aversion spreads out to include the whole course of things in this world. In his first soliloquy he sheds light on his repugnance towards that world:

> How weary, stale, flat and unprofitable
> Seem to me all the uses of this world.
> Fie on't, ah fie, 'tis an unweeded garden
> That grows to seed, things rank and gross in nature
> Possess it merely (1.2.133ff.).[7]

7. Dutch translation of this passage.

The degenerate state of affairs in the Danish garden (Hamlet is vexed as well by other national abuses, such as immoderate drinking) is a catalyst for a general complaint that the world is an empty wasteland. One should not mistake his attitude for a romantic *Weltschmerz*, or the nausea Sartre proposes. Hamlet's feelings of frustration are colored by moral concerns. The vacuity and defiance of reality flow from immorality. That comes to expression in the image of the unkempt garden.[8] The good herbs are suffocated by the weeds that are not pulled out when they should be, and the whole garden becomes an unnatural and offensive place.

For the spectator, the theme of the sense of unrighteousness and ambiguity of morals becomes clearer by means of what plays out between the triad of Ophelia, Polonius, and Laertes. The response of Ophelia to the directions of Laertes, who offers a moralizing speech, is telling:

> Do not as some ungracious pastors do,
> Show me the steep and thorny way to heaven,
> Whiles like a puffed and reckless libertine
> Himself the primrose path of dalliance treads,
> And recks not his own rede (1.3.47ff.).[9]

In the light of this interchange, it is for both an effrontery when Polonius addresses his son, who is ready to take his leave for another country, with this cliché: "To thine own self be true" (1.3.78). What is the "own self," and what is it to be "true" in a world pervaded by moral ambiguity?[10] For Hamlet this ambiguity is exemplified even more clearly later in the play. What is the love of Ophelia worth, if she so casually breaks her agreement? What is his own life worth, if apparent love can so easily serve as a cloak for lust? What is friendship worth, if his supposed friends, Rosencrantz and Guildenstern, are so willing to be manipulated by the king? Nowhere, it seems, can one find a solid footing on which he can build a life. Behind decorous behavior and polite conversation, passions come to dominate: the pursuit of a luxurious life, sexual promiscuity, pleasure seeking, vanity, and self-interest—these are the vices that have taken over this world.

8. The image of the neglected and wild garden comes frequently to Shakespeare. Cf., inter alia, *Richard II*, 3.4.37ff.

9. Dutch translation.

10. Heinrich Heine writes in his *Deutschland: Ein Wintermärchen*: "I know the manners, I know the text, / I know also the deception of the gentleman / I know you secretly drink wine / and publicly you preach water."

The dramatic situation is heightened when the ghost appears as a reminder that a murder has been committed. Hamlet becomes convinced of his suspicions: "O my prophetic soul!" (1.5.40). Beneath the superficiality and sham, we hear a horrifying truth. A murder has been perpetrated. It is the early sin of the murder of Abel by Cain, which drew upon it "the primal eldest curse" (3.3.37) who vented his suppressed anger against his brother.[11] A murder is something other than passions. It is a shocking, knavish deed. The life of the Danish court plays out on the pivot of a secret murder.

What Is to Be Done?

The real theme of *Hamlet* is neither the murder nor the ambiguity of the underlying moral intent of the play. It is, rather, What must I do? The first, universal question is this: What is the appropriate bearing of a person in a world that is, so to speak, *an unweeded garden*? The more specific question is this: What must you do when you know that a murder has been perpetrated against your father? The complexity of *Hamlet* lies right here—that the general motif is entangled with the specific one. The answer to the second question cannot be detached from the first. The idea that this world is so dominated by the weed of the passions is so benumbing that one knows not where to begin and, thus, nothing gets done. This sense of impotence so paralyzes Hamlet that he would rather raise his hand against himself and end his life:

> O that this too too solid flesh would melt,
> Thaw and resolve itself into a dew,
> Or that the Everlasting had not fixed
> His canon 'gainst self-slaughter. O God, God (1.2.129ff.).[12]

Suicide can flow from several motives, as so often appears in Shakespeare's tragedies. The topic of suicide is very conspicuous, at least as a motif, in each of the tragedies. For Hamlet, the motivation is the escape from reality and the accompanying loathing he experiences. He rules out suicide, however, permanently. God has forbidden it. God's unqualified

---

11. Shakespeare often refers in his plays to the murder of Abel by Cain. Cf. what concerns Hamlet himself in the scene in the graveyard, where a gravedigger uncovers the skull of some politician and where Hamlet comments: "How the knave jowls it to the ground as if 'twere Cain's jawbone, that did the first murder" (5.1.65).

12. Dutch translation.

command keeps him from the act; otherwise he would have decided to raise his hand against himself in the act of suicide. Hamlet is no Roman, for whom God's command against suicide has no force.[13] He will obey the command. Life is a gift that may not be refused. The right of self-determination is checked by these limitations. However, this command is external, and Hamlet does not really internalize it.

Whenever further in the play the option of suicide threatens, it is, again, the religious-based inhibition that checks Hamlet against the deed. There is the famous passage that begins with "To be or not to be" (3.1.56). Otherwise than in the first soliloquy, the question this time is whether all the misery and grief of life is to be endured. "Who would fardels [burdens] bear, / To grunt and sweat under a weary life . . . ?" (3.1.76ff.). Why not "take arms against a sea of troubles / And by opposing end them" (3.1.58ff.)? But Hamlet takes into account the divine judgment after death. To the question why one is not to make an end to his life, the answer is "the dread of something after death" (3.1.78).

It is this thought "that puzzles the will" (3.1.80). Fear of final judgment holds men prisoner in this world, with all its misery. In terms of one's self-respect, that is certainly not a desirable situation:

> Thus conscience does make cowards of us all,
> And thus the native hue of resolution
> Is sicklied o'er with the pale cast of thought (83ff.).[14]

Conscience, nevertheless, lies close to knowing: it is the inner witness that distinguishes good from evil. His thought is in tension with the idea of what might follow after such an act. The hazards of transgressing the law are too great. It is fear which imposes restraint. One does not trifle with God. It is wiser to forego the experiment than to take the chance of learning whether the reward is truly applicable. The price, however, is great. Thus, man becomes a coward. It is this schizophrenia that needs to be resolved. Hamlet, thus, confronts his doubt: should he take his life, he will have displayed the courage to put an end to the humiliating attitude of submissiveness to frustration and immorality, but he then runs the risk of eternal damnation. Should he choose not to do so, he will have shown respect for God's commandment and will have escaped judgment, but he

---

13. Cf. *Macbeth* 5.8.1ff., where Macbeth speaks about "playing the Roman," is mentioned in connection with suicide.

14. Dutch translation.

is then compelled to endure what is beyond endurance. And that is a form of cowardice. What would restrain a man from suicide should he dismiss concern about the final judgment? It is not surprising that such a person as Albert Camus should consider this question the philosophical theme *par excellence*.[15]

Finally, Hamlet does not need to make a choice. There is work to be done, as it appears. In place of ending his life, he receives the summons to take revenge. But is Hamlet really obliged to kill Claudius? What can be said for doing so, what speaks against it? What is the state of the dilemma? On the one hand the obligation is present for the son to avenge the wrong done to his father. But is that sufficient warrant? There is a character in *Hamlet* who, indeed, affirms such an obligation. That is Laertes. As he comes to learn that *his* father has been killed, he shoves all considerations and ethical concerns off to the side, including any thought of a divine judgment:

> How came he dead? I'll not be juggled with.
> To hell allegiance, vows to the blackest devil,
> Conscience and grace to the profoundest pit!
> I dare damnation. To this point I stand,
> That both the worlds I give to negligence.
> Let come what comes, only I'll be revenged
> Most thoroughly for my father (4.5.130ff.).[16]

Laertes declares that he will permit nothing to stand in the way of avenging his father. The obligation for revenge is an absolute duty. Neither vows nor relationships, neither mercy nor pity, nor the possible consequences of a similar deed in this world or the next, will deter him from his resolve.

It is obvious that Laertes' attitude exhibits a pagan worldview.[17] Here is talk about revenge without scruples. Such an attitude would not emerge in a culture informed by Christianity. Laertes is reverting to a pre-Christian code of honor ethics. The honor of the family has been besmirched, and now Laertes needs personally to avenge this insult. From a Christian perspective, such an ethic is at least dubious and affords no opportunity for the exercise of justice and grace. Laertes sweeps all such

---

15. See especially *Le Mythe de Sisyphe*.

16. Dutch translation.

17. Laertes's earlier admonition to Ophelia, where he enjoins her "be wary then, best safety lies in fear" (1.3.43) is at odds with this passage.

considerations off the table. He even agrees later to become complicit in a cowardly plot to kill Hamlet.

This pattern of Christian norms and values can, in various ways, shove aside this legacy of Christian ethics. Laertes does so through reverting to an earlier, an "unbaptized" code of behavior. Shakespeare provides us with other examples, such as the enlightened person, one who devises his own creed by appealing to "nature." Edmond, in *King Lear*, exemplifies such a person. He addresses nature as his goddess (1.2.1). In the light of the service of nature, any notion of moral principles present in the culture gets shoved aside. This is the Machiavellian man who, with contempt and scorn, claims superiority over the childlike Christian codes and, in his overweening self-esteem, borrows the notion of the right of the strongest. Whoever, in his opinion, exercises restraint derived from a traditional Christian culture is a menial drudge.[18]

Ethics of honor and Machiavellianism have in common the heavy emphasis in the value they place on the virtue of courage. They stand in contrast to the cowardly, those who do not dare to oppose the existing moral codes. One is tempted to ask whether this position does not transform courage into something else. Courage can also be a component of other value systems. There is evidence that courage can endure evil and see clearly what is present without one's fleeing ignobly from the scene.[19] It takes courage in a world of injustice not to quietly choose to end one's own life. It takes courage to resist the will to power. It is a nefarious bias to designate an attitude of life that is based on obedience to a command, as cowardice. Obedience to law, provided that it is not a slavish imposition, generates its own face of courage.

Hamlet is too much a Christian to uncritically choose the code of revenge, although at first he seems to tend that way. Once Hamlet encounters the ghost, he undergoes a change and is delivered from his melancholy. After the ghost disappears, he says:

> And thy commandment all alone shall live
> Within the book and volume of my brain
> Unmixed with baser matter: yes, by heaven! (1.5.102ff.).

18. See, for example, Geach, *The Virtues*, 151.

19. Obedience in Christian ethics is not to be interpreted as blind obedience to authorities. I refer here to the splendid passages of Karl Barth contained in his *Kirchliche Dogmatic*, II. 2, 612–701. Cf. also the surprising essay by Noordmans, "Mystiek in de moraal," 357–66.

From this day on there is but one mandate, and that is the commission to inflict revenge. There is but one mandate, and that is the obligation to avenge the murder of his father. No other thought is to occupy his mind.

So Hamlet, just as was true for Laertes, starkly confronts the temptation to understand this one-sided view of courage as the readiness to harbor thoughts of revenge in order to carry out the deed itself. He reproaches himself for his irresolution:

> Why, what an ass am I! This is most brave,
> That I, the son of the dear murdered,
> Prompted to my revenge by heaven and hell,
> Must like a whore unpack my heart with words,
> And fall a-cursing like a very drab,
> A scullion! (2.2.535ff.).[20]

It does not occur to Hamlet at this moment that his reservation against a blind rush for revenge is prompted by an objective norm of right and wrong. He rebukes himself because he is comparing himself with the model of sheer strength , driven by passion (from an actor, besides). Elsewhere he blames himself for not being a great person who is inclined "to find quarrel in a straw / when honour's at the stake" (4.4.55ff.). This also, however, is a temptation, since, to quote a character from another play, "'Tis mad idolatry /T o make the service greater than the god."[21] Action in itself is no virtue. He wants to overcome his irresolution with the words, "Oh from this time forth, my thoughts be bloody or be nothing worth" (4.4.65).Hamlet rightly enters a danger zone. This is the disposition of Macbeth, who has discarded all positive impulses and feelings while he is translating his resolve into deeds.

Hamlet is persuaded at certain moments of the rightfulness to kill Claudius and to avenge the murder of his father. When he does so, however, he does not do so because of rejecting the notion of God—his command or his judgment—still less by the igniting of his passions—but, rather, on the grounds of insight into the very nature of justice.

> . . . is't not perfect conscience
> To quit him with this arm? And is't not to be damned
> To let this canker of our nature come
> in further evil? (5.2.67ff.).

20. Dutch translation.
21. *Troilus and Cressida*, 2.2.53ff.

It is not just killing the murderer, who in the name of divine and earthly justice must be put to death, that will bring about Hamlet's own condemnation. So is also the *perfect conscience* that prompts him to the deed. *Conscience* here is meant to designate not only an inner awareness, but also knowledge based on a good insight into the true moral order. Now, this insight into the moral order does not throw a moth-eaten veil over the deed, but it helps one to carry out the task.

This awareness, however, comes only after a long process. Hamlet must assure himself that he is acting in the service of divine justice. Should that not be so, then his act of revenge will only make the misery that much the worse. The first burning question that demands an answer is this troubling one: From whence does the ghost derive? The danger is great that the ghost has emerged from the inferno. Can such a ghost be safely trusted?

> ... The spirit that I have seen
> May be a devil—and the devil hath power
> T'assume a pleasing shape. Yea, and perhaps,
> Out of my weakness and my melancholy,
> As he is very potent with such spirits,
> Abuses me to damn me (2.2.551 ff.).[22]

Hamlet doubts the credibility of the ghost. What sort of ghost are we dealing with? His doubts mirror those of his contemporaries. For both Roman Catholics and Protestants, appearances and supposed messages of the ghosts were considered very dubious. People were urged not to trifle with them. Small wonder that Hamlet's companions prevented him, in the first act, from pursuing the ghost. In *Macbeth* they appear as witches. They speak the truth, just as the ghost speaks the truth, but it is ultimately a fatal truth, which destroys Macbeth. This world is at least problematical, and Hamlet's mission is no less dubious. It is no sign of cowardice, therefore, that, while he acknowledges his mission, he wavers before the task. His hesitation is anything but cowardice; it springs from a mature Christian conscience.

Hamlet's problem is not only ascertaining the status of the dubious appearance of the ghost. He faces a still deeper problem. The world is complex. Who is the scoundrel, who is the victim? Do I know for certain the true state of affairs? Can I be sure whenever I draw my sword that I will not be striking the wrong person? Am I being led by a benign ghost,

22. Dutch translation.

so that my motives will be genuine and so that I will preserve my honor and my conscience afterwards? The blood of so many supposed scoundrels has already flowed that one might think there are no bones left to bleach. Have I let myself be lured by an errant ghost? Have I mistaken windmills for giants and murderers for innocent citizens? Have not my own deep frustrations skewed my sense of reality? Such is the real problem of Hamlet. That he feels deeply as he faces these questions speaks well of him.

And now for a second question. Is the mandate really to be carried out? Which mandate does he eventually take upon himself? There is far more to do than avenge a murder. In the tragedy, Hamlet also gets assigned the task of bringing to light the rottenness of the world. Once he is helped along the way by the ghost, he sees himself as the *scourge and minister* (3.4.173), an agent of heaven. He is the avenging justice, appointed to scourge, respectively, Polonius, Guildenstern, Rosencrantz, and Claudius. They are all questionable characters. Each of them will meet his death at the hands of Hamlet. He also acts to arouse the voice of conscience in Claudius and Gertrude.

Hamlet, thus, is "the scourge and minister," the executor of divine justice. It has all to do not only about the vacuity of the world but also about the moral bankruptcy of people who put up a good front but who secretly are driven to give vent to their evil passions This *scourge and minister* understands his commission as one given by divine appointment, as assigned by providence. After he has killed Polonius, Hamlet says to his mother:

> . . . For this same lord,
> I do repent, but heaven hath pleased it so,
> To punish me with this, and this with me,
> That I must be their scourge and minister (3.4.173ff.).[23]

His role as scourge of God pervades the play. The remarkable scene set in a graveyard in the beginning of act 5 must be understood in the light of divine judgment. It is as if a universal accounting is taking place. The gravediggers are digging a grave for Ophelia, and, as they do so, they find and toss skull after skull, blithely hacking them with their spades. Hamlet and Horatio watch them at their work, imagining as they talk to which of various groups of people each skull might belong. The first is that of a statesman, who would even lead God around the garden if he could; but

23. Dutch translation.

he is in fact a murderer, because his skull is Cain's who committed the first murder. The second is a courtier, who uses his intrigues, tricks, and machinations to advance himself in the world. The third could be that of a lawyer, who has enriched himself through the jargon of his trade. The fourth is Yorick, a jester, who has done nothing more in life than play the fool. Hamlet assigns Yorick one more errand—to "go to my lady's chamber" and warn her about the final disposition of her painted face. It is a macabre scene, comparable to the porter scene in *Macbeth*. It is as if doomsday has arrived. The purpose of this scene is to serve as a mirror for the whole play. The first skull, that of statesman, is linked to Claudius. The second reminds us of Polonius, as well as Osric, who is about to make his appearance in the next scene. The fifth of the skulls points to Ophelia and Gertrude.[24] All are drawn to their destination; everything moves towards the final end of the fifth skull: the lady's, not yet consummated.

Hamlet regards himself as the scourge through whom the heavens are inflicting judgment. He also calls for judgment on his former friends, Rosencrantz and Guildenstern, whose death awaits them. This drives him to rise at night and locate the room of the two friends in order to uncover the plot against him. Providence has also seen to it that Hamlet possesses the king's seal, so that he was able to sign the death warrant for his turncoat friends: "Why, even in that was heaven ordinant" (5.2.48).

A one-sided preoccupation with Hamlet's inner feelings and thoughts has often left untreated this other side of Shakespeare's tragedies, with the result that the element of divine punishment is often, though not always, overlooked. The world is really full of rot, and the tragedy serves as a sort of judgment day. It is not that judgment is limited to the dire lot of the victims; rather, a more universal judgment is taking place, and Hamlet does not escape this judgment either. However dubious the occasion may be, that Hamlet is God's scourge, which is sweeping through the play and without which the play would have little worth, is obvious. There is but one just man found and spared in the play, and that is Horatio. It is worth noting as well that, at the play's conclusion, Horatio is the only survivor.

Hamlet and Conscience

There remains still another side. Hamlet may be seen objectively as the executor of justice, but by regarding him in this way we run the risk of

24. "I have heard of your paintings too" (3.1.137).

not paying enough attention to the history of Hamlet's inner life. Hamlet is a document of sorts, registering a wide range of feelings and thoughts, and it is difficult to ascertain who or what is the true Hamlet. Because of the length of the tragedy and its decelerating pace, the action leaves room for the development of Hamlet's inner life. That life, however, is not an orderly one. Ophelia laments this turbulence when she says about Hamlet:

> Oh what a noble mind is here o'erthrown!
> . . . Now see that noble and most sovereign reason,
> Like sweet bells jangled, out of time and harsh (3.1.144, 151 ff.).

Bells that ring out of tune—so Hamlet's mind appears in its disorderly outbursts. And this is in addition to his "antic disposition," his supposed madness. He strikes false chords. But as has been made clear, it is not this restlessness that underlies his contempt for man and the world, as he says to Ophelia: "What should such fellows as I do crawling between earth and heaven? We are arrant knaves all, believe none of us. Go thy way to a nunnery" (3.1.124ff.). Men are villains who should be banished, and women are well advised to shield themselves by entering the cloister. He had said earlier to Rosencrantz and Guildenstern: "What is this quintessence of dust? Man delights not me, no—nor woman neither. Dust, matter—that is man's destiny, high and low, and not even Augustus Caesar will escape this fate" (2.2.290ff).

As has been made clear, just as Hamlet on the one hand sets forth a negative and bitter attitude towards life, on the other hand he tends to brute revenge. He regularly airs his bitter attitude against life: "To be honest, as this world goes, is to be one man picked out of ten thousand" (2.2.176ff.). Honesty is hard to find, everything is a mere pose, or camouflage, behind which passions conceal themselves. This reflects a cynical view of reality, and Hamlet is radical to the point where he questions his own motives and accuses his very self. One thinks of the voice of the prophet Elijah from the Old Testament: "O Lord, take away my life, for I am no better than my fathers" (1 Kings 19:4). After the contest with the priests of Baal and the rebuke to the irresolute nation, doubt also besets Elijah even after he strikes down the skeptical priests. And that, then, is also precisely the other side: the danger of declining to commit the act of revenge. There is a moment in which the urge to inflict revenge almost leads him to the deed. The context in which this urge comes once again strongly resembles Macbeth before he commits the murder of Duncan.

'Tis now the very witching time of night,
When churchyards yawn, and hell itself breathes out
Contagion to this world. Now could I drink hot blood,
And do such bitter business as the day
Would quake to looke on. Soft now, to my Mother:
Oh heart, lose not thy nature; let not ever
The soul of Nero enter this firm bosom.
Let me be cruel, not unnatural (3.2.349ff.).[25]

This is a dangerous statement. Hamlet knows well enough how to ward off a blow, and it is there that the voice of his conscience speaks, but the underworld casts its shadow over him. Is it the arrival of the ghost? Are we faced with the appearance of the dubious ghost, on whom Hamlet has sworn to take revenge? Later, Hamlet will run his sword through Polonius, and after that, he adopts a reckless state of mind.

The tragedy of Hamlet is that of a self noble of soul but who, supposedly mandated to rid the world of evil, oscillates between self-contempt and misanthropy on the one hand and bloodthirstiness on the other hand. As Hamlet sees Claudius kneeling in prayer, Hamlet backs off from killing him, for in the posture of prayer Claudius might well escape the hell he deserves.

Hamlet is a sensitive soul, noble, of high birth, possessed of great intellectual gifts. One seldom sees the breadth of such a mind. He is heir of a rich moral tradition and is disposed to honor important intuitions of the Christian faith. He is the son of a gallant father. He distinguishes himself in a positive way in his environment. But Hamlet is also a lonely figure. He does have a friend, Horatio, but that does not offset his solitary mien. All this is fascinating about Hamlet. A man comes on the scene who has been cut off from the meaningful institutions of land and family. That has happened through no fault of his own. He is away from Wittenberg (he would otherwise have become a scholar) and is forbidden to return. His relationship to his mother has been severed, and to the throne is held off. He is "a floating individual." He is not so by nature. He prizes friendship, is committed to the country's traditions, and has had a close relationship to his father and mother. This man is now being confronted with injustice flowing from a murder and with the chaos that ensues from a diseased court. He becomes a lonely man. His several monologues also testify to his situation.

25. Dutch translation.

Is this severance of traditional relationships an image of the times? The stage always provides, as Hamlet himself says to a visiting group of players, "the very age and body of the time his form and pressure" (3.2.20). They are the "abstract and brief chronicles of the time" (2.2.481). Hamlet has indeed become a cult figure, a model of the individual man.

How does Hamlet reflect the world in which the lot of Elizabethan England is cast? Reputable historians call attention to the changing mindset of this era. The religious tensions and entanglements, the social transformation, the economic alterations—these were also the cause of the greater responsibility that now confronted people in their choices.[26] One need not put only a negative interpretation on this development. Instead of speculating too much about a possible Protestant context of *Hamlet*, let me say this. I am certain that the increasing emphasis on the individual as he wrestled with his own conscience was consistent with the Protestant emphasis on one's personal relationship to God. This shift brought about a deeper life of the soul. A man no longer relied on the intermediate agents of institutions and seasoned rituals; now he stands as an individual directly before God. It is not, however, that the man could proceed by his own compass. The word of God is his proper compass, and the proclamation of the gospel makes the word of God operative. However, man appropriates this message as an individual. He must answer for himself, and only such an answer is one freely arrived at. He must in freedom make the word of God his own. It involves faith (*sola fide*), and that points directly to the promise of God in the gospel. This will foster far more tension in the soul of the individual than was true in the traditional Roman Catholic Church. A new appreciation arises for the depth of the individual soul as he wrestles with his conscience in order align himself perfectly with the calling of the word of God. Gardner says as much when she observes, "Hamlet is a Christian tragedy in the sense that it is a tragedy of the imperatives and torments of the conscience." It needs also to be said that the term "Christian" has its proper place in the "musical composition" of Protestantism, though this is not to deny that it is applicable as well to other branches of Christendom.

Hamlet does not, as already stated, eschew religion. It is impossible to understand him apart from his religious affirmations. He achieves the legitimacy as avenger from the prevailing injustice and also from the voice

---

26. See, inter alia, Jones, "Shakespeare's England," 39.

of his conscience. However, his religion provides a one-sided view—a negative orientation. The compass needle is fixed on the *south-south-east* direction (cf. *north-north-west* in 2.2.348) in the direction of justice. But this direction point is very limited, and apart from that, it is difficult to maintain it consistently. The divergences in Hamlet's thinking all revolve on that point. Hamlet misses insight into the broader dimensions of religion. The word *grace* does not appear to be part of his vocabulary. Religion to him provides a motive for revenge. Hamlet also nourishes a fascination for death. Such is hardly a motivation for life. Life has dealt harshly with him, and he has not yet discovered the spur of God's kindness, except late, for Horatio only. The love of Ophelia could have served as such a channel, but he brutally rejects her, after but one absence. It is significant that Hamlet, though possessed of a religious nature, never prays. After the confrontation with the ghost, he promises Horatio, "Look you, I'll go pray" (1.5.131), but he does not do so. Another pregnant moment presents itself when he says to his mother: "Confess yourself to heaven, repent what's past, avoid what is to come" (3.4.150), but here again he lets disgust and cynicism dominate this last advice to Gertrude. It must be admitted that the fate Hamlet encounters hardly opens up other possibilities, but the notion that "there is a divinity that shapes our ends" points only to the dead. Would he have acquired a different understanding of "divinity" had he gone to Wittenberg?

Observations

The world of *Hamlet*, for all its brilliance, is an oppressive domain. No allusions appear to the source of goodness and truth, the realities that liberate. The sword is unleashed and does its work, but is it possible to live in a world in which the highest form of justice is revenge?

I have two situations in mind, both of which furnish a vision for a new beginning. Permit me to name them. In my judgment, they are crucial for an understanding of *Hamlet*. The first is a fragment, in the beginning, when the guards are confronted with a ghost. The ghost apparently wishes to speak, but as a rooster crows, it disappears.

> Marcellus: It faded on the crowing of the cock,
> Some say that ever 'gainst that season comes
> Wherein our Saviour's birth is celebrated,

This bird of dawning singeth all night long.
And then, they say, no spirit dare stir abroad.
The nights are wholesome, then no planets strike,
No fairy takes, nor witch hath power to charm,
So hallowed and so gracious is that time.
Horatio: So have I heard, and do in part believe it
But look, the morn in russet mantle clad
Walks o'er the dew of yon high eastward hill (1.1.156ff).[27]

The cock is the morning's messenger which sends the ghost fleeing. This cock is fitly placed, in terms of the birth of the Savior, Jesus Christ. Then all ghosts must withdraw, and all erring spirits become deprived of their powers. The night is wholesome, and the time is gracious and blessed. In this poisonous atmosphere a light radiates in acknowledgment of the Savior's birth. Not so incidentally, what follows hard upon can well be regarded as one of the finest images of the entire play.[28]

The birth of the Savior is a positive occurrence. A gracious power emanates from it. It is one of the few instances in which an image of God is clearly evident, one which enlightens the listener. It is a vulnerable passage, and it is not difficult, in a production of the play, to subject it to ridicule. However, it is this passage which refers to a remarkable episode. Does this narrative not point to an important truth? The birth of Christ always throws light on the incarnation of God. It is the feast of the coming of God into flesh.

The reference to the birth of Christ in a passage which speaks of a "strange eruption" (1.1.69) and of a ghost is striking. It throws light on his birth. The birth of Christ is not a romantic tale which transpires in the world of shepherds, sheep, and angels. Rather, it is placed in the decadent world of Denmark. It is an event which restrains the underworld and which creates daylight.

We get a second situation which also runs the risk of being interpreted ironically and, when done so, seriously interferes with a proper understanding of *Hamlet*. It is the high moment when Claudius for the first time permits the crime he has committed to truly pierce his heart. It is remarkable that Shakespeare, who has so far portrayed Claudius as a cunning statesman, now shows him as a vulnerable man unburdening his soul:

27. Dutch translation.
28. Dutch translation.

> Oh my offence is rank, it smells to heaven;
> It hath the primal eldest curse upon't,
> A brother's murder. Pray can I not
> Though inclination be as sharp as will.
> My stronger guilt defeats my strong intent,
> And like a man to double business bound,
> I stand in pause where I shall first begin,
> And both neglect. What if this cursed hand
> Were thicker than itself with brother's blood,
> Is there not rain enough in the sweet heavens
> To wash it white as snow? Whereto serves mercy
> But to confront the visage of offence?
> And what's in prayer but this two-fold force,
> To be forestalled ere we come to fall,
> Or pardoned being down? (3.3.36ff.).[29]

Of all people it is Claudius, a murderer, at the point of a life-changing conversion. And this requires *repentance*. The reaction of Claudius takes place after the production of *The Murder of Gonzago*. Here we encounter an example of a tragedy that elicits a stark moral response on the part of the audience, a reaction following a discovery. Claudius reminds himself that the power of mercy is available. The beautiful image "Is there not rain enough in the sweet heavens to wash it white as snow?" exerts a strong and moving effect on the scene.

A way is possible to reverse his plight: "Try what repentance can. What can it not?" (3.3.65). The way to attain mercy and the way of repentance is by prayer. This advice also gets expressed in moving language:

> Bow stubborn knees, and heart with strings of steel
> Be soft as sinews of the new-born babe
> All may be well (3.3.70ff.).

Let me observe in passing that, in my opinion, only an author who has an affinity for these concepts can devise such a portrait.

Claudius, however, cannot pray: "Pray can I not" (3.3.38) But oh, what form of prayer / can serve my turn?" (3.3.51). There follows the depressing conclusion:

> My words fly up, my thoughts remain below.
> Words without thoughts never to heaven go (3.3.97ff.).

---

29. Dutch translation.

Claudius's experience is the same as Macbeth's, later: "But wherefore could not I pronounce 'Amen'?" The way out to penance and the serious attraction to grace are nullified by a failure of will. Claudius explains that his soul is *limed*, imprisoned, as a bird is trapped by the lime on a tree branch. The possibility for a realistic breakthrough, thus, is squandered. A dark pall spreads over Claudius and, ultimately, over the whole play. That is ultimately the source of the depressing heaviness of the play: where the world of forgiveness and renewal is beyond reach, the human drama remains unresolved. There is good reason for the depressing conclusion: "The rest is silence."

5

Macbeth

MACBETH IS ONE OF the shortest of Shakespeare's plays. The text, which reaches back to the so-called Folio edition of 1623, probably contains some additions of Thomas Middleton (1580–1627).[1] The play was written about the year 1606, three years after the Scottish king James VI was crowned in 1603 as King James I of England. The timing for a play set in Scotland could not have been coincidental. The material which he used he obtained from *Holinshed Chronicles, Part II*, which narrates the history of the Scottish royal line. But one should also remember that Shakespeare takes liberties with his sources. Shakespeare wrote *Macbeth* presumably after *King Lear* and before *Antony and Cleopatra*.

Macbeth is a play enveloped in night and darkness. It evokes a world of horror and fear. It is also the most concentrated of Shakespeare's tragedies. With *Hamlet* and *Othello* (also the earlier tragedy, *Romeo and Juliet*), it transpires in a Christian world.[2] The central event is the murder of the sitting Scottish king Duncan, which Macbeth carries out with the help of his wife, Lady Macbeth. The murder is conceived in the first act. Macbeth as commander of the Scottish army, has put the enemy (a combination of armed forces from the Hebrides, Norway, and a traitor) to rout, and on his return from the battlefield he meets with witches who prophesy that he will become a king. Macbeth and his wife resolve to give these

---

1. Co-authorship was a normal occurrence in Shakespeare's time. The last plays, *Henry VIII* and *The Noble Kinsman*, are most certainly co-authored plays. One may assume that the other plays attributed to Shakespeare are indeed his work. The additions in *Macbeth* concern acts 3, 5, and 4.1.39–43 (and possibly 125–32).

2. Of the other tragedies, three are set in the Roman world (*Julius Caesar, Antony and Cleopatra, Corolianus*), one in the Greek (*Timon of Athens*), and one in pre-Christian England (*King Lear*).

prophets a helping hand. The murder takes place in act 2. Duncan's sons, Malcolm and Donalbain, flee respectively to England and Ireland. The murder of Banquo, friend of Macbeth and cousin of the king, takes place in act 3, after Macbeth has been crowned king. Macbeth senses that Banquo represents a danger to his only recently attained crown. But Macbeth next sees the ghost of Banquo at a banquet and reacts in terror. Another highly placed noble, the Thane of Fife, Macduff, flees to England, leaving his wife and children behind. Act 4 shows forth the reign of terror Macbeth launches. The nadir occurs when Macbeth kills the wife and children of Macduff. Meanwhile, plans coalesce to liberate the land from Macbeth's tyranny. The last act shows the actual liberation of Scotland and the downfall of Macbeth. On the basis of the soothsayers' predictions, Macbeth supposes himself invulnerable, but the reality plays out very differently. Macduff kills Macbeth, and Malcolm becomes the new king of Scotland.

This narrative generates a number of themes, which are theologically of great importance. The play is in that sense one of Shakespeare's most Christian plays. I will explain in the following pages some of these aspects, all of which circle around the mystery of evil.

Temptation

Macbeth commits a murder. That deed does not come to him willy-nilly. Although our first impression of Macbeth is that of a bulldozer who has flattened his enemies, he is not a killing machine without scruples about murdering the king. Macbeth needs first to be tempted, and not until he succumbs does he commit the murder. The temptation of a protagonist is an important motif in many of Shakespeare's plays, especially in the tragedies. The temptation presents itself as an alluring possibility, one that appeals to deeply cherished desires and secret intuitions. The question becomes whether the protagonist will give way to the temptation. He is not compelled to do so; he can resist the temptation. Man is not a mere plaything in the hands of an inexorable fate. He is a player, and however he may be overcome by circumstances, there remains always leeway to exercise his freedom. Circumstances and character provide the possibility and the allure, but they do not force the decision. That is why, in the tragedies, the reality of guilt comes into play. The tragic motif does not shut out the moral issue. Shakespeare leaves no doubt that the choice for evil is alluring and attractive and that the tragic figure gets ensnared by it. None of this, however, eliminates his responsibility for his doom. Evil lays snares for the soul of man, and to the spectator his fall seems necessary (and for the progress of play, also unavoidable), but there is no talk of sheer necessity.

The "tragedy" of the tragedies, has, among other elements, to do with the status of the man who experiences his downfall. Macbeth possesses a strong personality. He has noble dispositions. We learn in the second scene of the first act how he bore himself as a hero in the battle against the combined forces arrayed against King Duncan of Scotland. Duncan praises him as a "valiant cousin! worthy gentleman!" (1.2.24) and "noble Macbeth" (1.2.69). He is not only gallant, but humane by nature. According to his wife, he is "too full o' the milk of human kindness" (1.5.17). She knows him as a man of ambition, whose goal, however, does not permit of just any means to achieve it. "What thou wouldst highly, that wouldst thou holily" (1.5.20). He would prefer to realize his deepest cherished wish in a manner where the end does not justify the means. He is no mere scoundrel who is being tempted, but a man who evokes sympathy. In this respect *Macbeth* differs, for example, from *Richard III*. That historical drama about kingship is not, in fact, a tragedy. It is a play about a king who from the very outset says, "I am determined to prove a villain" (1.1.30). There are scoundrels whose downfall comes not only in the hour of their temptation but who are evil all the way through and serve as agents of the devil. There is a swarm of such characters in the plays of Shakespeare. They personify evil. One thinks, besides Richard III, of such figures as Aaron (*Titus Andronicus*), Edmund (*King Lear*), and Iago (*Othello*). This description, however, does not apply to the main characters in Shakespeare's tragedies.

But the other side must be kept in mind as well—that Macbeth, though not an evil person, is tempted because he is open to temptation. He has not distanced himself from evil. Evil, in the form of desire, has its bridgehead in him. He desires to become king: that is his hidden ambition, even though he knows that the kingship would not normally accrue to him, but to the oldest son of Duncan, Malcolm. He has already taken the first step on the journey to convert the wish into the deed itself because he has intimated as much to his wife (1.7.47). In consideration of the character of Lady Macbeth, who is no less ambitious to become queen

(Macbeth must surely have been aware of her desires), he is playing with fire. His hope that his life will proceed on "the swelling act / of the imperial theme" (1.3.128ff.) is the handle of the power of the temptation.

Counter Forces

Since man is subject to temptation, life turns out to be a dangerous affair. What is easier than for a form of desire to fasten itself in the human heart? And how likely that this desire will become inflamed and that the thought becomes a deed? In a fallen world there is a legion of occasions for desire to pass over into action. Still, many sound reasons are on hand to keep temptation from getting a hearing. When the three witches on the heath, the so-called Weird Sisters, prophesy that Macbeth will become king, and when Lady Macbeth welcomes this news and Macbeth challenges the witches with objections, Macbeth is well restrained by many reasons to withhold consent to the temptation.[3] He sums this up himself: he is related to Duncan through blood and as subject of the king; Duncan is protected by the obligations of hospitality that accrue to a guest; Macbeth acknowledges that his guest is a highly-principled man (1.7.12ff.); and human justice will not permit the criminal to go unpunished. Macbeth acknowledges that a moral order exists that one cannot lightly shove aside. There is an order based on reality that is reflected in common law and positive law and that serves as a dike against evil.

This "conservatism" is an important element in human life; it prevents the world from becoming a haunted house. Scotland will be plunged into chaos once Macbeth comes to power and carries out his tyrannical acts. And all just because this conserving principle is swept off the table. A brutish will to power turns life into a nightmare: "Unnatural deeds / do breed unnatural troubles" (5.1.68ff.).

It does appear that nature itself is endowed with an innate morality. As Macbeth commits the murder, he prays first that the "sure and firm-set earth" (2.1.56) will not hear his steps. He commits the deed at the moment when "nature seems dead" (2.1.50). Reversed, unnatural behavior destroys the natural order. In a conversation between one of the Scottish nobles and an old man, after the death of Duncan, these words get said about the disturbances in nature: "Tis unnatural, / Even like the

---

3. About the world of these Weird Sisters, see below.

deed that's done" (2.4.10). Darkness overcomes the day, and a hawk is swallowed by an owl. Also, Duncan's horses, beautiful and swift, "turn'd wild in nature," and "contending 'gainst obedience" (2.4.16ff.) break out of their stalls and devour each other.

This power of disorder is invoked even more strongly when Macbeth, still uncertain of his position and as yet restrained by the "remnants" of the existing moral order, seeks out the witches. He adjures them to speak, even if that would involve an assault on the whole order of nature and "the treasure / of nature's germens tumble all together" (4.1.58). The "germens" about which he speaks are the invisible seeds that, according to St. Augustine, constitute the groundwork of the visible and material realities of creation.[4] Macbeth will annihilate these and thus create a world no longer based on firm laws and necessary structures but, rather, as if in the hand of a great manipulator—in this case, Macbeth himself. One is prompted to speak about an extreme individualism, where reality no longer has any structure and where everything material will be subject to an arbitrary, despotic will.

The irony of *Macbeth* is that in the end it is precisely Macbeth himself who appears to have counted too much on the firm structures of the world. The witches predict that he cannot be killed by anyone who is born of a woman, and that he can be overcome only when the forest of Great Birnam starts walking toward his castle on the hill of Dunsinane. Trusting in the way things ordinarily are, Macbeth considers himself invulnerable—but in vain. Macduff, it appears, has entered the world through a caesarean operation, and Macduff gives orders to his men to cut boughs from the trees to conceal themselves. Thus, the forest does indeed come walking to Dunsinane, and Macbeth perishes. It turns out, then, that even the evildoer must reckon with a normal and good order. From that point of view, the consequences of the evil acts are contradictory. Those acts aim to destroy order that, once destroyed, nullify the possibilities to perform the evil. Thus viewed, evil turns out to be parasitic to the good.

Back to the theme of temptation. Summing it up, we find on the one hand a powerful force attracting man to evil and, on the other hand, we see that the world is not a snake pit. Shakespeare's tragedies exhibit well how fragile is the natural order, and how, by itself, it fails to provide a safe

---

4. See among others Augustine's *De Genesis ad litteram libri duodecim*, 6.5.8. The idea comes via Plotinus from the philosophy of the Stoics. See among others, Coppleston, *A History of Philosophy*, 2.1.91ff.

basis for man, but it is inaccurate to ascribe a pessimistic world vision to him on that account. However dark the night in which life disappears, the day will return, whereupon life can resume its normal course.

The Form of the Temptation

Man encounters temptation in a structured world. That world poses a strong barrier against evil. How, then, does the temptation break through this barrier? It is worth noting that this occurs via a logic that assumes the form of morality. Against the moral considerations that Macbeth cites, as listed above, Lady Macbeth posits an alternative morality. She supposes that Macbeth is a divided personality, a person who harbors desires but stops short of acting them out, a trait which points to a lack of valor and to cowardice. She reproaches him for the moral inconsequence of a person making an assertion but on whose word one apparently cannot count. That deficiency will inevitably bring about a painful lack of self-respect ("and live a coward in thine own esteem" 1.7.43). She challenges him to become "a man" The devil appears as an angel of light (2 Cor 11:14). The moral logic of the tempter is a powerful weapon capable of removing one's scruples, and it appears that Macbeth is no match for his wiles. The suggestive power of these influences uses attractive images and plausible reasons to make the cause represent a higher morality than the "burgher morality" which Macbeth is displaying. The virtues of bravery, trustworthiness, and sense of honor are brought to bear on Macbeth to overcome his scruples.

It soon becomes apparent how ambivalent morality is. True and false morality cannot easily be distinguished from each other. Moral rationalization can bend any which way. Moreover, they may have a poisonous background. "A truth that's told with bad intent / beats all the Lies you can invent."[5] Moral arguments are not without merit, but in practical life they don't serve as a reliable standard. It is not for nothing that a key word in *Macbeth* is *equivocatur* (2.3.9). An equivocator is one who will deliberately convert words into double meanings, someone who, under the guise of good, will reach out towards the evil. The word *equivocator* is a clear reference to the morality of the Jesuits.[6] There is a form of moral

5. Blake, "Auguries of Innocence."

6. In 1605 the so-called Gunpowder Plot took place, an attempted attack on the king

deceit, which at first glance cannot be distinguished from true morality, and people, sometimes unthinkingly, can easily be seduced down the path of evil ways. There is a casuistry that is ultimately based on false grounds. "Fair is foul and foul is fair," so we hear at the very beginning, and it becomes the motto of the whole play. The human heart is deceitful, and that also threatens the human community. "There's no art / to find the mind's construction in the face" (1.4.11ff.). One can, alas be mistaken on first sight. Somebody may even be mistaken about his own honesty.

Ultimately the question is not one of moral reasoning but whether the heart is pure. Thus, a wise man responds to certain kinds of reasoning as Banquo did when, tempted, he said, "But hush; no more" (3.1.10). Taken on a deeper level, what matters is a heart and a life—a life that is anchored in the higher order of God's grace. That is the only counterforce that is a match for the temptation and that can distinguish between a deceitful and a pure moral argument. Shakespeare leaves no doubt that the source of morality ultimately rests in that domain.

The Reach of Temptation

Before I proceed further, I need first to point out that the theme of temptation does not apply only to Macbeth. We catch other protagonists opening themselves to temptation—Malcolm, son of Duncan, among them. I will pass him by, however, and turn attention to two figures who belong to the lower classes. Even though his tragedies always revolve around the upper classes, often folk from royal blood, Shakespeare does indirectly give the lower classes their due.[7] In 3.1 it becomes clear that Macbeth wishes to dispose of Banquo. Along with Banquo, Macbeth has defeated the enemies of Scotland. Banquo has also encountered the witches and heard from them that his descendants would inherit royal honors. For

---

by means of casks of gunpowder planted in the space under the House of Lords, where the king was about to open a session of Parliament. The attack was justified by a dubious moral reasoning: The pope had excommunicated the king of England, and the king could thus be regarded as a usurper. The plot failed. A legacy of deep suspicion lingered long in the aftermath of the event.

7. Erich Auerbach points to the mingling of the high and low styles brought about by the Christianity-inspired literature of the Western world. He maintains correctly that Shakespeare stands in this tradition of the Middle Ages, and in his plays resisted his opponents who wished to distinguish the high and the low styles. Auerbach provides a brilliant example in *King Henry IV, II*; see *Mimesis*, 314–36.

this and other reasons, Macbeth sees him as a dangerous rival who must be put out of the way. He cannot do this himself, since he cannot yet be sure of the security of his own position. He hires two commoners to carry out the task. They are not coerced to commit the crime. Macbeth has to persuade them.

That these two men are seduced comes about because they belong to the world of people who feel that they have been oppressed and exploited by the higher classes. They have suffered the "vile blows and buffets of the world" (3.1.108) and seethe with resentment and hate. These "gut" feelings are grist for the mills of Macbeth's aspirations. He assigns a name to these oppressors: the name of Banquo. And so they become murderers. They take guilt upon themselves.

They do not do this lightly. It takes an extended argument for Macbeth to win them over, as can be seen from the intensity and length of his speech (3.1.74–107, 113–125). He has imitated the art of his wife by using quasi-moral arguments to win them over. Macbeth challenges them to be "men"—men of character who are resolved no longer to endure the curtailment of their rights. Noteworthy is that this "ethics of man" turns against another ethic. Macbeth asks them:

> . . . Are you so gospell'd,
> To pray for this good man, and for his issue
> Whose heavy hand ow'd you to the grave,
> And beggar'd yours for ever? (3.87ff.).

Obviously, the morality of "being a real man" contends with the morality of the gospel. Unwittingly, Macbeth has here named the source of true morality: the gospel. This morality prompts men indeed "to pray for this good man." In a subtle manner, to our surprise, a gospel truth emerges here as a source of morality, as we find in Matthew 5:44, where Jesus says, "Love your enemies and pray for those who curse you." It appears as if precisely among the lower classes the morality of the gospel has found a foothold. People are so influenced by the gospel that they will prefer enduring wrong to committing murder. It is high drama that Macbeth propagates himself as the pseudo-leader and well-wisher of these people. He breaks them loose from the influence of the gospel by his "morality of the masters." Resentment can be overcome through the morality of the gospel or, conversely, can be amplified in the deed of extending the hand to beat down the neighbor.

The Porter Scene

The centrality of the theme of temptation is once again highlighted by a remarkable scene, one that, though omitted in many productions, remains crucial to an understanding of the play. This is the so-called porter scene, which occurs in scene 3 of act 2. The guard at Macbeth's castle is roused early in the morning after the murder by a pounding on the door. At that point he imagines that he is the gatekeeper of hell. Perhaps Shakespeare used this reference because in some medieval interpretations hell was portrayed as a castle guarded by a porter.

The banging on the door goes on for some time, and with each knock on the door the porter surmises what sinner is knocking, which one has given in to a form of evil for which he has obviously not atoned. He first sees in his mind's eye a farmer who was so set on gain that he hanged himself when the price fell because of overproduction. The second is a Jesuit (called an *equivocator*), who committed treason for God's sake. The third is an English tailor who stole the French fashion and cloth. Because of the cold, the porter breaks off this series, but he had planned "to have let in some of all professions, that go the primrose way to th' everlasting bonfire" (2.3.19ff.). His plan was to introduce representatives from all the callings, folk who perished because they yielded to temptation and took the primrose path strewn with flowers, but who actually arrived in the eternal fires of hell.[8] This strange scene places the murder of Macbeth in a broader context; every profession, it seems, has its own allurements. It is as if the castle of Macbeth, where a murder has been committed, is a collecting place for all sorts of transgressors who, one by one, have lacked the power to resist their specific temptation. Their sins spread out like an oil stain. Who can escape?

The porter scene is an important intermezzo, one which makes you think that the play is not only about a bizarre murder by an evil Macbeth but that it is about a theme that concerns everyone and also one that will multiply the thoughts of the spectators.

8. In *Hamlet* a comment appears about "the primrose path of dalliance"—the frivolous, flowery path of rollicking merriment which leads to destruction. Cf. also the expression "the flowery way that leads to the broad gate and the great fire" (*All's Well that Ends Well* 4.5.50ff.), remarkable for being placed in the mouth of a buffoon. It's the representatives of the lower class who give us their commentary on the misdeeds of the high and mighty. It is precisely in their commentary that we can most clearly hear the voice of the poet.

The Metaphysical Background: "Murth'ring Ministers"

The temptation of persons can for the most part be understood in terms of ordinary moral categories. Still, Shakespeare offers another dimension. The temptation does not occur as a simple interaction between human beings.

It is not by accident that *Macbeth* is set on the heath near the battlefield where three witches appear simultaneously, expecting to meet Macbeth, who has just won a battlefield victory. Later, the witches are called Weird Sisters. These are ghosts who have insight into the "seeds of time" and can therefore predict the future. They have antecedents in the figures of the goddesses of the Fatum, the so-called Fates. That they are not merely neutral beings becomes very clear by their being designated as "witch." An obvious bond exists between them and the power of evil.[9] They are spirits from the nether regions who intend to lead people into evil. Clearly, there are powers present in the world that aim at human beings and wish to ferry them to their downfall. For Shakespeare and his contemporaries the devil and demons were real and not to be trifled with. That is what makes *Macbeth* such an engaging play. It is Banquo who accurately sums up the nature of these witches:

> And oftentimes, to win us to our harm,
> The instruments of darkness tell us truths;
> Win us with honest trifles, to betray's
> In deepest consequence (1.3.123ff.).[10]

The Weird Sisters offer him a double prophecy, of which one has just been fulfilled. They are soothsayers, aren't they? The Weird Sisters "tell us truths." It is a prophecy of a kingship. But they drive Macbeth into a direction that will eventually lead him to murder. They have as their goal "to betray's in deepest consequence." They employ a dangerous equivocation (5.5.43). Too late does Macbeth realize this, when it appears that their

9. For what concerns Shakespeare here, I am in agreement with the observation of Curry, *Shakespeare's Philosophical Patterns*, 61, who states that whether one considers these hexes human witches who are in contact with the powers of darkness, or as demons in human form, or as lifeless symbols of evil, the powers that they exert, represent or signify, are demonic. Many warnings were issued in Shakespeare's time against demons and hexes. King James I wrote a *Daemonologie,* in which he provides a comprehensive view of the demonic strategies. See also for the theme of demonology: Nijenhuis, "Over Heksen, demonen en demonologie: Shakespeare's *Macbeth,* and the demonology of Jacobus."

10. The author provides a Dutch translation of these lines.

further predictions are ambiguous and treacherous; they are spirits "that palter[11] with us in a double sense" (5.8.20). They promise a seeming good in order to ruin a soul. In the words of Macbeth: "It has cowed[12] my better part of man" (5.8.18). The evil spirits know with what bait they must catch the heart because they can read the hidden desires of a man, and whenever the victim jumps at the bait, he is dragged to destruction. He is a "fiend, the common enemy of man" (3.1.68).

Does all this imply that the fall of Macbeth is finally owing to necessity? This question has the more relevance because of the fact that the Weird Sisters can see into the future. If the future is fixed, how much freedom is available to Macbeth? What can a person do when there is obviously a form of predestination, a reality that cannot be altered?

This question has always received much attention in discussions about God's foreknowledge. In the theological literature of the sixteenth and seventeenth centuries, the mainstream has always taught that God's predestination does not obstruct human freedom. God's knowledge in advance what anyone will do does not compel him to do anything. God knows in advance what a person is going to do in freedom. The foreknowledge of God does not function as a blocking force that makes it impossible for a person, say, to mend his or her way or to resist evil.

More than that, the prophecies of evil cannot be equated with those of God. God's foreknowledge is infallible, that of the ghosts, not. One should not believe their words, far less place one's trust in them. Macbeth, however, is prompted to proceed because the prophecies that he heard were promptly fulfilled. The latitude his will enjoys becomes greatly threatened. He could have stuck with the conclusion he originally drew from the prophecy that he would become king, namely, "If Chance will have me King, why Chance may crown me without my stir" (1.2.142ff.). From that prediction he really does not need to set up a plan of action. He need not intervene to further the conclusion of the prophecy.

But the words work out in a different way. Obviously a man "in himself," sprung loose from other forces that would restrain him, is defenseless against the whisperings of evil. The fatal moment occurs when Macbeth's trust in these whisperings become set. Banquo had suggested that as well in his commentary on the prophecy of the "witches: that

11. palter—that is, juggle.
12. cowed—that is, dispirited.

trusted home . . ." (1.13.120). The evil force demands a man's total *trust*. When that is achieved, disaster results. Nowhere can it be determined precisely at which moment this fatal trust was born. Was it there first, to be activated later? Was it given at a later time? The moment of the fall cannot be traced.[13] However it happened, Macbeth capitulates. He can offer no resistance against the deceit that teases him with the attractive promise of the kingship.

Once having fallen for these promptings, his freedom diminishes even more. In fact, the actual commission of the murder of Duncan is no longer a free act. Macbeth enters Duncan's room finally by following what he sees as a dagger. It is an apparition, something more than a mere image. It is also the action of evil enacted in his mind's eye. It is as if he were drawn with a cord in order to do the deed. Having once committed the murder, the possibility of making further choices is finally extinguished completely. He becomes a machine bent on murder.

Lady Macbeth invokes these instruments of darkness herself. Apparently, human nature—in spite of all its susceptibility to evil—is not capable of committing certain sins without the instigation of the evil one. The passage where she invokes the evil spirits is of great importance:

> . . . Come, you Spirits
> That tend on mortal thoughts, unsex me here,
> And fill me, from the crown to the toe, top-full
> Of direst cruelty! make thick my blood,
> Stop up th' access and passage to remorse'
> That no compunctious visitings of Nature
> Shake my fell purpose, nor keep peace between'
> Th' effect and it! Come to my woman's breasts,
> And take my milk for gall, you murth'ring ministers,
> Wherever in your sightless substances
> You wait on Nature's mischief! Come, thick Night,
> And pall thee in the dunnest smoke of Hell,
> That my keen knife see not the wound it makes.
> Nor Heaven peep through the blanket of the dark,
> To cry, "Hold, hold!" (1.5.40–54).[14]

13. Cf. the analysis of Kierkegaard in *Het Begrip Angst*, which shows a gap between the temptation towards evil and the deed itself, a gap which cannot be bridged.

14. Dutch translation.

There are, thus, spirits that "tend on mortal thoughts." They can bend these thoughts toward evil. They are "murderous ministers" eager to bring to life the seeds of evil in men and in nature and are prepared to bring these purposes to fulfillment. Human nature in itself, without external intervention, is not in a condition to commit gross evils.[15] For that, an intervention from satanic powers is necessary. These stand all too ready to take up residence in the thoughts and hearts of people. They transform men into monsters and obliterate the unique characteristics of human nature: *unsex me*. They especially shut out any entrance of the good, here designated as *compunctious visitings of Nature*, the compassionate promptings of human nature, and they fend off any divine visitations so that man becomes deaf to their voices.

In short, the murder which Macbeth commits would not occur without the influence of evil forces. The gothic aura of the play also suggests the power of evil. Human beings are too small to unleash so much terror. We are not on a par with evil forces that are rightly called "superhuman." All this is what accounts for the tragic character of the play. Lady Macbeth is not a devil incarnate either. By summoning the devilish powers, she goes against her own nature, as it will appear. A stark image used to dramatize the interaction between human action and demonic influence is that of the sale, or the transfer, of the soul to the devil. This traditional motif, which contemporary Marlowe took over in his *Doctor Faustus*, also plays a role in *Macbeth*. Macbeth talks about "mine eternal jewel" (3.1.67) that he has surrendered to "the common Enemy of man" (3.1.68), the devil. What he receives in its place is his goal—but as will become clear, a king in name only. His sinfully acquired kingship will prove to be an empty shell.

One can readily acknowledge as self-evident that spirits, murderous servants, and similar agents are part of Shakespeare's world picture. And it is true as well that for his purposes as dramatist he readily took over the earlier conventions that belong to the heart of his purpose with the play. We face here an issue not readily of solution and one on which I do not intend to expand. But we must take heed less everything in Shakespeare that is not in accordance with the world picture of modern man is viewed only as form, and that, thus, has nothing to do with the real content of the play and, therefore, neither with Shakespeare's own conviction—whose

15. This is in contrast with the angels. That is one of the reasons why in classical Christian theology the fall of the angels is final.

real conviction now miraculously happens to be in agreement with that of modern man. Such an approach avoids a confrontation with Shakespeare's work.

The Metaphysical Background: The Heavenly Power

Whenever the metaphysical background comes into play, one must avoid limiting the discourse to the demonic powers and influences. Other forces are active in the play, the heavenly. The case is this, that without a robust relationship with these latter forces, man is finally no match for the evil powers. Macbeth nowhere consults the heavenly agents. It is otherwise with Banquo, who also feels the attraction of the temptation. Moreover, Banquo overhears the prophecy of the witches. His heirs are to become kings. Obviously, the talk of these sorcerers must have aroused in him thoughts similar to those of Macbeth. But he designates these as "cursed thoughts" (2.1.9)—cursed because the witches' predictions also entice him to assist in their fulfillment. Banquo resists their temptations through prayer.

> . . . Merciful Powers!
> Restrain in me the cursed thoughts that nature
> Gives way to in repose! (2.1.8ff.).

It is clear that Banquo is directing his prayer to God. Because the government authorities had forbidden the use of God's name in dramatic performances, the circumlocution *Merciful Powers* is used instead. Elsewhere the word *Grace* is used (for example, 5.9.38, "the grace of Grace"). Because he has not locked up his thoughts within himself but opens himself to the heavenly powers, Banquo remains safeguarded against the suggestive power of the temptation. After the above-quoted words, he encounters Macbeth, who asks him if he in time will support him. Banquo is agreeable, though with conditions: "But still keep / my bosom franchis'd, and allegiance clear" (2.1.2ff.). He wishes to keep his conscience clear of guilt and his loyalty firm—that is to say, unblemished. It is not by accident that Banquo, after the murder of Duncan, when daylight arrives, says, "Fears and scruples shake us: / in the great hand of God I stand" (2.3.127ff.).

Macbeth refuses to consult the heavenly powers. He deliberately cuts himself off from them. That becomes apparent at the very moment he is considering whether to commit the murder. One of the considerations that arises in his mind is that of divine retribution and the accompanying eternal damnation. However, standing on the sandbank of time ("this bank and shoal of time" 1.7.6), he is prepared to risk the loss of life eternal ("We'd jump the life to come" 1.7.7). Only the fear of earthly justice can restrain him. As will become evident, even this fear is not sufficiently strong to finally stop him from committing the murder.

A dramatic moment occurs in the scene of the murder itself. When Macbeth finally goes to Duncan's bedroom, he sees there his two sons, Malcolm and Donalbain, half-asleep, half-awake. He later tells his wife what he encountered there:

> One cried, "God bless us!" and" Amen, the other,
> As they had seen me with these hangman's hands.
> List'ning their fear, I could not say, "Amen,"
> When they did say, "God bless us."
> Lady Macbeth: Consider it not so deeply.
> Macbeth: But wherefore could not I pronounce "Amen"?
> I had most need of blessing, and "Amen" stuck in my throat.
> Lady Macbeth: These deeds must not be thought
> After these ways: so, it will make us mad (2.2.26ff.).

Macbeth has cut off his ties with the source of blessing, God himself. He still feels the need of acquiring the blessing at the moment he has committed the murder, but the "amen" remains stuck in his throat. He can no longer get the word out. He has lost the power to pray and even say "amen." That is the first effect of the murder. He has lost the ability to do what the sons of Duncan do, "Say their prayers."[16] It is an illusion to suppose that a person can be safely anchored merely in a few humanistic virtues when confronted by the seductive force of evil that hides the dark abyss.

Divided Man: Macbeth

The profundity of this play lies especially in the psychological analysis of the nature of the murderers, Macbeth and Lady Macbeth. Man is a being of flesh and bone. Human nature is no neutral datum. Man has been created for life in community. His spiritual and physical constitution comes

---

16. Cf. Claudius in *Hamlet*, who wishes to pray after he has murdered his brother, but can no longer do so.

into its own when he displays the king-becoming graces: "Justice, Verity, Temperance, Stableness, / Bounty, Perseverance, Mercy, Lowliness,/Devotion, Patience, Courage, Fortitude" (4.3.92ff.). Should he deviate from these, he denies the deep intuitions of his own nature. It is no surprise that Macbeth's very body reacts violently when ambition to become king manifests itself and takes the form of a device to murder Duncan. The image of the murder makes his hair stand on end and his heart slam against his ribs. His whole being ("single state of man," 1.3.140) suffers from such an emotional shock that his cognitive abilities are suppressed and so that "Nothing is, but what is not" (1.3.142). That is, reality yields to what is not, and what finally appears not to exist. The physical and mental part of a human being show a definite defensive reaction to the invasion of evil. One might call this a morality of human life that has a firm physical base. Human nature is a nature created by God himself. Human nature permits an enormous variety ("the gift of bounteous Nature" 3.1.97), but it is not without boundaries. It becomes clear in *Macbeth* that man is not made of plastic material which can be formed as one pleases.

As suggested earlier, Lady Macbeth understands intuitively that she must, even more than her husband, alter her human nature in order to carry out her misdeed. She asks the sprits, "Unsex me" (1.5.41). She begs to be released from what it is that pertains to her human nature, even when it is involves transgression, namely, the access and passage to remorse. She wishes her breasts to give gall rather than milk. Women's breasts that provide milk for her children constitute a strong sign of the liberality of human nature and the generosity towards another, especially those who deserve their protection. Whoever then dams up this life-source to pursue the goal of personal ambition will inevitably supply gall in place of milk.

Just as in other plays, *Macbeth* poses the central question—the question about human nature. Who or what is man? Lady Macbeth wishes to transcend the form of humanity in her husband with a higher morality of humanity. She holds before him the perspective to be "so much more the man" than he is now. "Manliness," from which every trace of feminine tenderness has been expelled, will be required if he is to do the deed without the "boomerang" of fear and uncertainty which haunt ordinary people. Such a person is a sort of Ubermensch—a superman. And that reasoning obviously becomes contagious, as we see when Macbeth persuades the intended murderers of Banquo to cooperate with his plan, as has been described earlier. Macbeth challenges them with the perspective of being not only "men" (man) but to achieve a higher ranking of humanity, "not i' th' worst rank of manhood" (3.1.102).

Shakespeare was in his time confronted with an ideal of autonomy derived from the Machiavellian creed, which was known by that name.[17] In this ideal the strong man lives out of his own resources as contrasted with the masses—the crowds who are weak and incapable of autonomy. Such an attitude comes through very strongly in someone as Edmund (*King Lear*), but appears as well in the role of Iago (*Othello*). The tragedy in *Macbeth* is seeing how Macbeth as well as Lady Macbeth perish by this ideal of autonomy.

Machiavellianism is an extreme form of a turn in the thought about the human being as it came to the fore in the Renaissance. Central in this pattern of thinking is nature and whatever is natural. And this natural is disconnected from the supra-natural.[18] Machiavelli drew a radical conclusion from this, but in fact he built on the foundation that the Renaissance had laid. It seems that Shakespeare does the same in appealing to human nature. However, his very conflict with Machiavelli shows how carefully one needs to interpret the situation. When human nature is seen as autonomous, then the war over the interpretation of the character of this nature also breaks out immediately. Does the appeal to nature justify the choice Machiavelli made? Does human nature involve the language of justice and compassion? These are open questions, with which modern Western history would engage itself, like a shadow.

Whenever nature, however, is seen in a normal context, with a relationship to a reality beyond the natural, the case appears otherwise. In the Middle Ages the nature of man was relegated to a higher level. Nature is a given nature, one intrinsically endowed with a destiny. Nature proceeds from God's hand, and the natural is a gift which God has lent to man. And even when a person breaks away from God, he still remains susceptible to the influence of God and of his grace. Thus understood, nature is a reality that resists "unnatural manipulation." The natural opposes evil that is unnatural and, therefore, destructive. There exists an objective reality, and it is a blessing when a person remains attached to it.

---

17. See Spencer, *Shakespeare and the Nature of Man*. Cf. also Schneider, "Shakespeare and Machiavelli," 131–71.

18. See Veldhuis, *Een Verzegeld boek*, 28-36.

Conversely, evil and sin follow in the loss of contact with this objective reality. They launch man into a subjective world, which in increasing measure takes on the character of an unreal, ghostly universe. That becomes very clear, as well in the case of Lady Macbeth as with Macbeth.

The Divided Person: Lady Macbeth

It is a strange situation with Lady Macbeth. She is the tempter who incites Macbeth to commit the murder, and she high-handedly asserts that if he will not do it, she will do it herself. But at the very crucial moment she shrinks back from doing so. The sleeping Duncan bears too close a resemblance to her father (2.2.12ff.)! While she has boasted that she will murder her own child for the higher goal, she sees herself in an unexpected moment as her father's child. Once the murder has been carried out, she repeats her words as a refrain: "These deed must not be thought / after these ways: so, it will make us mad" (2.2.32ff.). The "What is done is done" rings like a charm to ward off danger, but these words ultimately appear not to work. When the ghost of Banquo appears, she is the concerned hostess who nervously attempts to rescue the bewildered Macbeth. Not much is left now of the fearless woman. She no longer responds to Macbeth's bravado to continue on this path of blood and murder; she wants only to pacify him with a weak "You lack the season of all natures, sleep" (3.4.140). After this she disappears from the stage.

She emerges again only in the first scene of act 5, a shadow of her former self. In the well-known sleep-walking scene it becomes clear that she has burdened herself with a load her human nature cannot carry. What is done is not done but continues on in her subconscious mind. Her soul has become prey to despair. Consciousness of guilt compels her to wring her hands to wash off the blood, but in vain: "All the perfumes of Arabia will not sweeten this little hand Oh!—Oh! Oh!" (5.1.47). As an accessory to the murder of Macduff's wife, she cries out with the well-known words: "The Thane of Fife had a wife: where is she now?" (5.1.40ff.).

The doctor who has been observing her concedes that her case goes beyond his competence. She has a heart that is "sorely charg'd" (5.1.50); it is one that is found in those who have "infected minds" (5.1.69): "More needs she the divine than the physician" (5.1.71). This is his last comment, after which he adds a prayer, "God, God, forgive us all!" It is as if he wishes to say with this comment that Lady Macbeth is no exception. The bystander (the doctor, but also the spectator of the play) can take little pride in his own virtue. Everyone needs forgiveness, and everyone needs to ask for forgiveness. Lady Macbeth has cut herself off from "access to the remorse" and is therefore a despairing soul. It is a soul that has handed itself over to the destructive powers of evil and has shut itself off from the source of grace. Her despair, so the doctor fears, may lead to suicide, and it is not by accident that rumors emerge that Lady Macbeth has ultimately ended her life by her own hand (5.9.36ff.).

The Divided Man: Macbeth

Macbeth's journey to ruin proceeds along another route. The consequences of his embarkation on the path of evil can be traced more clearly, and his fatal development comes into focus more sharply than with Lady Macbeth. In addition to the fear that afflicts him both before and after the murder, it is significant that at the end he is troubled by hallucinations. He sees a dagger whose handle, upon closer examination, has been flecked with blood, and it precedes him on his way to the room where King Duncan lies. But the dagger is not to be grasped. His senses of sight and touch are affected, the first sign that he is disengaged from reality and that another world has taken over.

A next indication is his sleep. Sleep gets described as "great Nature's second course." This benefit of nature is no longer Macbeth's to enjoy. Sleep is a spontaneous gift of nature. Duncan sleeps and, thus, serves as a model for a person who lives out of the springs which nature provides. The murder of Duncan is also a murder of sleep: "Macbeth does murther Sleep" (2.2.35). Sleep is "the chief nourisher in life's feast" (2.2.39). Sleep is, next to a mother's milk, the highest expression of nature's liberality, a gift which cannot be purchased and serves as the clearest evidence of heaven's generosity. Lady Macbeth and Macbeth murder the most important sources of this nature. How sterile life can become when the relationship with nature in her role as benefactor is severed will become evident. Macbeth will sleep once more, but his sleep will be punctuated by "terrible dreams," and Lady Macbeth suffers in her sleep, muttering the words "a great perturbation in nature" (5.1.9).

After the murder of Duncan, while everyone is in a state of confusion, the reaction of Macbeth is significant. True, he is pretending, wishing to show to others how deeply shocked he is, but he speaks without understanding the deep truth of his own lines: "For, from this instant, / There's nothing serious in mortality; / All is but toys; renown, and grace, is dead" (2.3.90ff.).

Macbeth has, with the murder of Duncan, also killed the qualities of respect and grace. He has cut himself off from the social factor of grace and the religious factor of grace. He has cast his lot for a world detached from honor and grace. This world is an empty world. His admission to the real world has also been cut off. This is the door of remorse and pity, but that door has been slammed shut. The ideas of penalty, repentance, and forgiveness he has banished from his universe. What remains is a person completely imprisoned in his own world.

This burnt-out void becomes even more evident at the end of the play. By that time he has become a totally hardened sinner, one who is no longer capable of the human emotion of fear. This capacity, however dreadful, is a normal reaction of human nature. This nature is slowly but surely being eviscerated. A complete insensibility has overtaken him. Then comes the news that his wife has died. These well-known words follow:

> . . . Out, out brief candle!
> Life's but a walking shadow; a poor player,
> That struts and frets his hour upon the stage,
> And then is heard no more; it is a tale
> told by an idiot, full of sound and fury
> Signifying nothing (5.5.17ff.).[19]

It is obviously absurd to suppose that we are overhearing Shakespeare's philosophy of life in these words. However beautiful the language, it does not prove that Shakespeare subscribes to this view. What they point to is "the state of a hardened sinner for whom the world has no more meaning."[20]

The image of life as a theatrical drama, by the way, has a long history, one that goes back to the ancients. Shakespeare has earlier placed such words in the mouth of the misanthrope Jacques in *As You Like It.*

19. Dutch translation.
20. Bethell, *Shakespeare and the Popular Dramatic Tradition*, 92.

However, Jacques does not have a very positive idea either about the act man is playing, for this stage actor ends his speech with "sans teeth, sans eyes, sans taste, sans everything" (2.7.139ff.). The rather melancholy verse of Jacques takes on a nihilistic variation in Macbeth's speech. He is experiencing the whole of life as a meaningless venture from a pitiful actor who leaves no footprints behind.

The stage imagery has also been used earlier in *Macbeth*. Since two utterances of the Weird Sisters have come to pass, Macbeth has a lively hope that the third will also be true. The two truths are "as happy prologues to the swelling act / of the imperial theme" (1.3.128ff.). This act now turns out to be anticlimactic. In a world which turns exclusively around Macbeth's ambitions, the whole play proves to be futile, and it dies like a candle in the night.

The horizon of meaning of the play, so crucial for a real culmination in a "swelling act," is missing, and, thus, the play descends into its own nihilism. It passes on, with all its ambition, all achievements, and leaves nothing behind. A meaningful world is always the given world, and an "I" is always the "I" we receive. But when one rejects what is given, its place is taken by a phantom world, a sham world and a sham narrative. This is not only a world without meaning; it is also a solitary world. Macbeth is king, but he discovers that he is a king without subjects.

In a world cut loose from nature and from grace, the search for an identity is an illusion, even if you are a king. Macbeth wishes to become a king, and he supposes that he will attain his true self as king. In his imagination he will then "be so much more the man" (1.7.51). However, he will no longer know himself after the murder. He does not recognize his own hands: "What hands are here?" (2.2.57). Lady Macbeth may then upbraid him: "Be not lost / so poorly in your thoughts" (2.2.70ff.), but he is doing just that—completely absorbed in his thoughts, and, thus, detached from reality. "To know my deed, 'twere best not know myself" (2.2.72). A wedge is driven between "I" and my deed.

Macbeth makes a contorted effort to continue on the road he has taken. The "I" attempts to adapt to the deed. The murder of Banquo constitutes training in the process of this adaptation. The training seems to misfire because Macbeth becomes terrified by the ghost. But since even here not a trace of repentance follows the deed, the hardening of his heart continues. The desperate person who is divided in himself and who desperately wants to be an "I" that he cannot be, becomes alienated from reality:[21]

> I am in blood
> Stepp'd in so far, that, should I wade no more,
> Returning were as tedious as go o'er (3.4.135ff.).

Turning back is surely possible in principle. Macbeth, however, has entered a stage in which meaningful decisions are no longer possible. Everything is shot through with weariness and despair. Freedom of action has dissipated in the absence of a meaningful world. Beyond this, Macbeth has so abused his freedom that it is about to expire. He has become a slave, a robot. He comes to this awareness too late. Too late also he learns that his true self has been destroyed by consorting with the "juggling fiends"[22] (5.8.19). He has lost his soul, his "better part of man." Macduff will kill someone who no longer has a soul, or a self, or freedom: "I'll fight, till from my bones my flesh be hack'd" (5.3.32). Macbeth had already announced this as well; there is indeed nothing more than that. If he is dead, he has been reduced to *a dead butcher*. His will has vanished; his feelings have evaporated.

Still, his fall is a tragic one. It does appear as if one flame of his original greatness manifests itself before his death. It is as if the courage that at one time was unquestionably his is a last reminiscence of the noble man he had once been. His death does not fail to leave a deep and lasting impression on the spectator.

Images of the Good

Macbeth is a dark piece, one infused with disaster and horror. It is a study in how evil courses through the life of a single man and a people. There is but little light in the play. Still, a few rays of light do break through in this dark world.

The most remarkable instance of goodness is offered by the English king Edward, "the most pious Edward" (3.6.27). As Macduff and Malcolm encounter each other in England, they get to hear about this king, who at that very time is taken up by a gathering of people suffering from the

21. Cf. also Kierkegaard, *Krankheit zum Tode*, who analyzes despair in its varying forms.

22. "Juggling fiends," defined in Dutch as "jonglerende vijanden."

plague and who expect healing from the king's touch. The ordinary healing arts have not been successful, but the people have vested their hope in the king, since "at his touch / such sanctity hath Heaven given his hand / they presently amend" (4.3.143).

This image of a king serves as a counterpart to Macbeth. The last time the subject of hands was mentioned happened after Macbeth's visit to the witches and his resolve that the "very firstling" of his heart will also be "the very firstling of his hand" (4.1.147). This hand will reach as far as the lives of Lady Macduff and her children. Where Macbeth sows death and destruction, King Edward extends his hand in healing. His hand is also a hand by which heaven itself brings healing. Where Macbeth stretched out his hand and knocked on the door of the witches, the king has knocked on the portal of heaven: "How he solicits Heaven, himself best knows" (4.3.49ff.). The word *solicits* puts us in mind of the *supernatural soliciting* of the witches in their meeting with Macbeth. The poisonous agenda of Macbeth is not the only influence at work in the world. There are also good forces. There is a gracious king who heals folk who are suffering from "The Evil" by placing a golden coin around their necks and offering a prayer with them. A beneficent world opens up. Besides his healing powers, he possesses "a heavenly gift of prophecy," a gift that one can regard as a counterpart to the Weird Sisters. The sickness about which this scene revolves is the so-called scrofula, a swelling of the lymph glands in the neck. It is worth noting that this sickness is called "The Evil," a detail that cannot but put one in mind of the parallel evil being enacted in Scotland.

In all the plays of Shakespeare involving kings, it is clear that the role of the king is a crucial one. A good king is a source of grace, while a bad king is a source of gall and bitterness. The king himself is not a god. He is no more than a mortal man, as becomes clear in *Richard II*. King Edward is not himself a source of blessing, but he draws from the true source of grace, heaven. And blessings descend from heaven on to the people. This same Edward is also prepared to assist the distressed Scottish people. Although Malcolm raps on the door of England like a beggar, King Edward offers him hospitality (3.6.24ff.). Subsequently he initiates forces opposed to the evil in Scotland—forces that ultimately produce good results. However black the night, it is the light of day that pushes back the night. Hell stretches out its hand to annihilate, but heavenly grace comes to the distressed to assist and procure justice for those without rights. The play also ends with the promise of a new era, one which will arrive through the grace of God (5.9.38).

The good in Duncan gives a somewhat weaker light. His character is not sharply drawn. He does not come through very clearly. He is actually more victim than actor. In the conversation between Malcolm and Macduff about the queen, Malcolm's mother, a momentary flash of light shines on the queen: ". . . The Queen, that bore thee / Oft'ner upon her knees than on her feet, / Died every day she liv'd" (4.3.109ff.).

The queen, it seems, had lived a life of prayer. She died every day, a practice which points to the daily dying with Christ. She is the queen who bore Malcolm, and Malcolm is the new king of Scotland, since the *butcher* Macbeth is now dead. We see, then, a few rays of light shine on the dark pages of *Macbeth*. They are few and marginal, but they are voices that point to the source of a renewal of life. It is possible to view these glimpses of light as mere tokens that contribute little to the meaning of the play. But the question remains on what ground such a vision can be justified.

6

King Lear

KING LEAR IS ACKNOWLEDGED by many as one of Shakespeare's greatest tragedies, next to *Hamlet* and *Macbeth*. It is a highly ambitious play with a great theme: human suffering. At the center of the play stands King Lear. Shakespeare probably wrote it after or before *Macbeth*, in 1606.

Shakespeare used a variety of sources for the story of King Lear and his daughters—among others, the *Historia Regum Britanniae* (from the twelfth century). The subplot, which revolves around Gloucester and his sons, Edgar and Edmund, he adapted from *Arcadia*, by Sydney. The tragic conclusion of the play, however, does not follow the sources which Shakespeare used.

Although the "real" narrative of King Lear is enacted in the "Christian" era, Shakespeare placed it in pre-Christian times. There is talk about gods, and Apollo and Jupiter are invoked. I follow the text edition of *The New Cambridge Shakespeare* and consider the text of the Folio edition as the basic text. I am not in agreement with the exegetes who uncover substantial differences between the Folio text and the Quarto text. For stage purposes, the text underwent changes, but this did not alter the essential text.

The play opens with the scene in which King Lear announces that he is about to divide his kingdom among three daughters—Goneril, Regan, and Cordelia. But he first desires a declaration of their loves. Goneril and Regan satisfy the king with flattering tongues, but the youngest daughter, Cordelia, provoked by these exaggerated and hypocritical declarations, does not follow suit. Thereupon the king curses and renounces her. The king of France, present in order to request Cordelia's hand in marriage, is not deterred by these curses but chooses Cordelia "for her very self" as his wife.

The play now exhibits how hypocritical were the declarations of Goneril and Regan. They quickly take exception to the pledge they had made to maintain Lear and his retinue of one hundred knights. The tension quickly increases to the point where they show Lear the door, an action approved by Cornwall, husband of Regan. It is night and the weather outdoors is beastly. In the subplot, a nobleman, Gloucester, permits himself to be set up by his illegitimate son, Edmund, against his legitimate son, Edgar. Edgar takes flight, disguises himself as a crazy man, and calls himself "*poor* Tom." He quickly discovers Lear. Tom and Lear are joined by Lear's jester and Kent. Kent is a noble whom Lear banished because he had defended Cordelia. He actually remains in the neighborhood of the king, in disguise. Now begins the "pilgrimage" of Lear towards a deeper insight into life.

Meanwhile, things do not go well for Gloucester either. He defends the king, but his bastard son, Edmund, betrays him to Cornwall. This barbaric man plucks out Gloucester's eyes. A servant cannot endure this sight and kills Cornwall; Regan, in turn, in a cowardly act, kills the servant. Gloucester, blinded, must now find his way to Dover. He is accompanied by his son Edgar, whom he does not recognize. Edgar remains disguised as "*poor* Tom."

Meanwhile it becomes clear that France is about to invade England. Cordelia, who has become Queen of France, instigates this action. She learns what Lear has to endure at the hands of her sisters and attempts to come to his aid. Cordelia finds her father before the disaster, and reconciliation takes place. Then the battle breaks out, with Britain the victor. Cordelia and Lear are taken prisoners. In the wake of all this, other events follow in quick succession. Albany, Goneril's husband, who had always opposed the machinations of Goneril and Regan, takes over the kingdom. Regan is poisoned by Goneril. A long history of tensions had existed between the two because both are in love with Edmund. Edmund, it comes to light, had intended to try to kill Albany, but he is unmasked through Edgar. Edgar then kills Edmund in a duel. Goneril, meanwhile, commits suicide. Edgar's father, Gloucester, has died as well, from the shock at the joy he experienced when Edgar revealed himself to his father. The play comes to a dramatic end. Edmund had issued a fatal order to have Cordelia hanged. Now Lear appears, with the dead Cordelia in his arms. His own death follows. Albany succeeds him as king.

Failed Fathers

King Lear is a drama of failed fathers. Lear casts off his daughter Cordelia. He abdicates his kingdom and proceeds to divide it among his daughters. His intent is to free himself from cares and "unburdened crawl toward death" (1.1.40).[1] Lear, thus, divests himself of his royal power in order to enjoy his old age. The unintended consequence is that he becomes a pseudo-king who must now live at the mercy and capriciousness of his daughters. This voluntary abdication is a form of dubious self-abasement. The one person who will not leave off from harassing Lear with his barbs is the court jester called "The Fool." Lear has not only arranged for his own comfort; through his division of the land he creates tensions and risks civil war. Thus, while serving his own interests, he endangers the lives of his subjects.

That, however, is not Lear's greatest blunder. That blunder lies rather in wringing the enforced declaration of love from his daughters. The greater the protestation of love, the greater the inheritance. By this act Lear interjects himself into the very center of his daughters' lives. He revels in the flattering speeches of Goneril and Regan and explodes in anger against Cordelia. She is a loyal daughter, which the king knows very well, but because she will not go along with "that glib and oily art" (1.1.226) of her sisters in their zealous expressions of love, Lear in his vanity loses his temper and banishes Cordelia.

Lear is not only the example of power which "to flattery bows," (1.1.149), but he also conducts himself as a degenerate father who curses his daughter, "without our grace, our love, our benison" (1.1.267). Kent also, a trusted servant, is banned whenever he challenges the arbitrary king. Through his self-love and vanity, Lear is so blinded that he labels Cordelia's and Kent's honesty a form of pride—a clear indication of how his judgment has become distorted. Obvious, too, is that Lear, whenever he turns to Kent, does so by invoking Apollo. Kent replies with these words: "Thou swear'st thy gods in vain" (1.1.162).

Thus, the play begins with the downfall of Lear. In other tragedies the time between the flawed act and the downfall of the protagonist is far greater. In *King Lear* they begin concurrently. In retrospect, though, the downfall resulting from his folly is clearly a foregone conclusion.

1. I am using the Arden text, third series. The textual tradition is very involved, but I do not intend to enter into a discussion of this matter.

And mark this, that the wicked sisters, Goneril and Regan themselves, acknowledge that by banishing Cordelia the king has shown "poor judgment" (1.1.292), though that, they say, is not surprising, since he "hath ever but slenderly known himself" (1.1.294). His rashness has erupted before this as well (1.1.297). Nevertheless Lear's deed confronts us with some form of *mysterium iniquitatis* (mystery of evil).

The downfall of Gloucester parallels the downfall of Lear. This revelation also occurs without preparation. Gloucester places a blind trust in the accusation that Edmund levels against Edgar. It can be said about Gloucester as about Lear that a precedent exists. He concedes right off at the well-known beginning of the play that he had dallied with an attractive woman and is well disposed towards the son, Edmund, born of this encounter. Gloucester's casual attitude towards his sexual escapade is a secret ulcer that has compromised his judgment. He lacks the ability to submit himself to self-criticism—and, besides this, suffers a form of self-love. No objective examination of Edmund's accusation gets carried out, and Edgar is at the same time placed under a death sentence. Gloucester is not a bad man, but even so a fallen one. One needs not engage in extensive moralizing to sense that these are failed fathers. This is the point of departure of *King Lear*. Those who are models of authority and nobility have fallen through the floor.

And great is their fall. They sin against those who are closest to them: their children. The child is a gift on whom the father has imposed his identity. The father is obliged, by nature itself, to exercise love and care for the child. Lear and Gloucester renounce their children, and, in the case of Gloucester, he actually sets in motion a plot for the death of his son. Henceforward they live as deficient fathers. "The king falls from bias of nature, there's father against child" (1.2.97). The result is degrading. They appear in the play as caricatures of themselves and serve as images of the "lost father."[2]

As the plot proceeds, they harvest what they have sown. Lear shuts his daughter out and will, in turn, be pushed out of doors by his other daughters. Gloucester first betrays, through his dalliance, his wife and, then, his legitimate son. He will be betrayed by the other son and will be deprived of the dignity of his fatherhood. Lear is locked out of his home

---

2. It is regrettable that Van Gennnep in his magnum opus *De Terugkeer van de verloren vader*, paid no attention to antecedents of this theme, which began in the late eighteenth century and, thus, spent no time with *King Lear*.

and, deprived of his mind, he flees half-naked outdoors into the night, exposed to the storm. Gloucester is shoved outdoors, sightless, having had his eyes plucked out. The insanity of Lear and the blindness of Gloucester are visual equivalents of their moral state. "Lear is mad" (1.1.147) Kent had said when he banished his daughter. And Gloucester will say it himself: "I stumbled when I saw" (4.1.21).

Both now see themselves as people imaged by Tom. They are no longer welcome in their own secure world, but, as failed people, they now associate with a fool. Seeing the fool, Lear recognizes in him the image of himself as well as man in general: "Unaccommodated man is no more but such a poor, bare, forked animal as thou art" (3.4.135). And this same Tom also gives Gloucester another insight into man, a view of whom, Gloucester says, "made me think a man a worm" (4.1.35). In a world of luxury and prosperity, it is very easy to adopt a flattering image of the situation, especially of oneself. This world is now being undone.

It turns out now that Tom himself is not only putting on a show as a poor duffer who sits half-naked in his hut. He is also a man who, by his own admission, finds himself in the grip of numerous demons. Is it coincidental that these fathers meet up with such a bedeviled man at this time?[3] The fact is that Lear—and in a certain sense this applies as well to Gloucester—are encountering a madman who asserts that he is being inhabited by many demons as punishment for his sins. The journey from the court and its flattering ways to the hut, and the talk of a madman who is seen as possessed by the devil, shows the free fall which has justly occurred to Lear. In the palace, this was the case: "They told me I was everything" (4.6.103). But in the hut he was told, "Take heed o' the foul fiend" (3.4.78). Well may Gloucester ask: "What, hath your grace no better company?" (3.4.138). And the answer needs to be: "No, and I deserve no better." *Ecce homo*. The dream of an all-powerful man who regards himself as the center of the universe is being cruelly destroyed. From this vantage point *King Lear* is a counterpoint to the parable of the prodigal son. That son repels his father, indulges himself and, ultimately, as is right,

---

3. For his account of Crazy Tom, Shakespeare made use of a book by Van Harneet, *A Declaration of Egregious Popish Impostures*, 1603. It is of little consequence whether Shakespeare concerned himself with demonology and whether or not he concurs with Harnett that the priests who performed exorcism were charlatans. The view of Greenblatt, in "Shakespeare and the Exorcists," 169ff. that Shakespeare is adopting the position of the Roman Catholic priests, is a typical example of recent pillorying of the text.

joins the hogs in the pen but may not even eat the food that the pigs eat. The son without the father loses his humanity and descends to the level of the animal. Conversely, the father who indulges himself but without, or opposed to, the daughter or the son, descends to the level of the man described as a "poor, infirm, weak and despised old man" (3.2.20). He can only be reinstated as he becomes once more the father of the daughter or the son. Moreover, that can happen only through the initiative of the daughter or the son as one or another is inclined to do so. Squandered fatherhood needs the infusion of radical grace. Where the father rejects his natural relationship of daughter or son, he requires the presence of a more than natural intervention emanating from the compassion of the daughter or son. Only in this way can reconciliation be achieved or a semblance of wholeness be restored. That is the somber truth which lies hidden in the narrative of *King Lear*.

Greatness in Suffering

Although Lear falls and finds himself at the mercy of his capricious daughters, he remains a great figure. His fall is great because it is the fall of a great man. His misery is great because it concerns a man who possesses great dimensions. The violence and greatness of the storm mirrors the violence and greatness of Lear. There is a "tempest in my mind" (3.4.12) as violent as the storm. Charles Lamb has put it correctly: "The greatness of Lear is not in a corporal but in an intellectual dimension . . . the explosions of his passion are terrible as a volcano; they are storms turning up and disclosing to the bottom that sea, with all its vast riches. It is his mind which is laid bare."[4] No ordinary man caught in a storm elicits the reaction that we witness in Lear. The madness of Lear is something other than the madness of a mere "*poor* Tom." It is the madness of one who was once but is no longer a king. His fall prompts one to think of the great judgment day itself. Gloucester's reaction as he encounters the king is to say, "O ruined piece of nature, this great world / Shall so wear out to naught" (4.6.130). It is a touching picture when Cordelia first meets him raging wildly out of control, "mad as the vexed sea, singing aloud" (4.4.2), decked with wild flowers. Again, *ecce homo*. It is not a good interpretation, it seems to me, to play Lear as

4. Lamb, "On the Tragedies of Shakespeare," in *The Works of Charles Lamb II*, 26.

simply a weak and mentally disturbed man. Misery and greatness must somehow be blended if the image is to be effective. Shakespeare shows this fallen man in magnified form. Lear's former greatness may be read in his present suffering and, in his madness, a remnant of a powerful reason or the possibility that he will regain this reason. Some may be inclined to use these actions as evidence of Shakespeare's humanism, but on deeper probing we must refer them to a Christian understanding of man. The misery of mankind is the misery of a great lord: the misery of a dispossessed king.[5] It is the image of God that has gotten into him in stormy weather. The wasted lives that Shakespeare creates are not the wasted lives of pitiful souls. There are such feckless creatures, too; the fawning Osric is one example. But these are marginal figures who, through the wrath of Kent, are held up to ridicule and are of little dramatic importance. These die also without any suggestion of heroism.

The protagonists in Shakespeare's tragedies are royal figures or people in high places. In them the image of man is displayed. The condition for tragedy is the "dignity of the fallen."[6] That condition becomes a problem in drama of the middle class, especially when the idea of an intrinsic nobility comes under attack. And in a time when characters are used as voices for nihilism, meaninglessness, hollowness, and vacuity, then tragedy becomes impossible. Shakespeare's noble characters, both in their suffering and decline, bring to mind the nobility of man of which Psalm 8 speaks: ". . . Thou hast made him little less than God." Where these notions vanish, very little scope for tragedy will remain. The fall of a noble animal is less thought-provoking than the fall of one of God's own children.

The Instrument of Suffering

However true it is that the fates of Lear and Gloucester can be attributed to their own failures, the fates are of a most horrible sort. Goneril, Regan, Cornwall, and Edmund are, each one, black characters. The fact that Goneril and Regan develop problems with their monthly turns to maintain the chosen knights may be understandable; it is doubtful, however, that they tell the truth when they accuse this contingent of debauchery. The manner in which, with their frigid attitudes, they denigrate the king and

5. Pascal, *Pensees*, fr., 116.
6. Aldus Lesky, cited by Balthasar, *Theodramatik I*, 406.

insist that he dismiss his whole retinue, rouses suspicion. The grossness of their crime lies in the hard-heartedness with which they force Lear and his followers outdoors. It is Gloucester who provides the sharpest commentary on their actions as he says to Regan "I would not see thy cruel nails / Pluck out his poor old eyes; nor thy fierce sister / In his anointed flesh stick boarish fangs" (3.7.55ff.). Those who are acting like the fangs of a wild boar will at a later point gouge out Gloucester's own eyes. As Lear deals with the unleashed storm outdoors, Regan cynically observes that this is the way self-righteous people might come to their senses. Goneril and Regan exhibit not a trace of compassion. They progressively harden their heart against their father. Their sin is not so much their ambition and search for power but their utter lack of compassion. Just as Lear had sinned against the Cordelia who had loved him, so these daughters sin against their father who had given each of them half of his kingdom. They thrust him outdoors and wish him dead. The final criteria by which characters are to be judged are love and compassion, or the absence thereof.

Goneril and Regan increasingly come into conflict with each other. The country of evil appears to be a country divided against itself. Goneril, the first of the two, poisons Regan. The apple of discord, except for desire for absolute power, is their mutual love for Edmund. Goneril will not shrink from killing to reach one's goal. The will to power and sexual delight drives them to commit murder.

Edmund is a more complex figure. He initially exhibits a sharper profile than Edgar and will not elicit any sympathy from the spectators. Nevertheless there is no doubt that he lives out of a principle that is ultimately one of self-destruction. The morality and ethos of an aristocratic society are matters for which he has no concern whatever. He acknowledges only the power of nature—at least as he understands it. Gloucester had followed his own natural lusts when he committed adultery. Edmund has been endowed, as he himself asserts, with a well-formed body and with a lively and witty spirit. Those are his assets, and he will exploit them to the fullest as he confronts the world. He has no compunctions about eliminating either his brother or father in order to achieve his own goals. Such "naturalistic" people play for high stakes and almost win. According to Danby,[7] Edmund reflects the mentality of the Machiavellian man of the new age who breaks with the conventions of traditional society, and, in

---

7. Danby, *Shakespeare's Doctrine of Nature*.

a time of loosening of traditional values, travels solely by his own compass, without regard to any moral scruples. He resembles Iago, in *Othello*.[8] These Machiavellian men exerted a strong appeal in Shakespeare's day. In a world in which old barriers were cracking at the seams and a new age was announcing itself, men were thrown upon their own resources. Those who came to London to seek their fortune were required to develop self-awareness, dexterity, and flexibility. In such a context a type of person can emerge who holds to the opinion that the end justifies the means. *The Jew of Malta* and *Tamburlaine*, by Marlowe, which featured such characters, achieved great success on the stage.[9]

One instance, however, can be adduced that will momentarily generate sympathy for Edmund. It occurs at the end when, while mortally wounded, he displays a humanitarian touch that is absent in both Goneril and Regan. One appreciates his protest against certain conventions. Moreover, this "real pagan" appears to harbor undeniable attractive characteristics. Shakespeare knows how to capture people's attention—as is, for that matter, also the case with Iago. Shakespeare himself may have been intrigued by Edmund. However, his self-seeking is the dominant principle, and, moreover, he strings together one intrigue after another. His end is, therefore, inglorious. When the news of Edmund's death is reported to Albany, he replies with this scathing comment, "That's but a trifle here" (5.3.294). He is carried off stage, dead—as are Regan and Goneril, and without a shred of pathos or dignity. He who lives by nature will perish by nature, in silence. Where existing laws construe man as only a well-endowed and well-formed animal, with "the survival of the fittest" inscribed on the statue books, there a person's death is no more than a "trifle," no more than a leaf blowing in the wind. His identity will disappear; he will be *carried away, like a dog* (Kafka). "When his breath departs, he returns to his earth; on that very day his plans perish" (Ps 146:4). Not because of his birth, but because of his actions, does he become *base, base.*

Although *King Lear* on the one hand contains enough potential for self-correction, of a self-complacent aristocratic order, and although in general it can be said that Shakespeare is by no means an author who writes to flatter the holders of power, it must also be said, on the other hand, that Shakespeare, in the character of Edmund, clearly permits us

---

8. Cf. also the chapter on *Macbeth.*

9. See also Ackroyd, *Shakespeare, de Biografie*, 148ff.

to see the consequences that follow when people do what they wish and flout laws and conventions.

The Suffering

The attention given above to morality as carried out by the actors should not let us lose sight of the fact that *King Lear* is, above all, a play portraying the suffering of man. An early dramatic high point is reached when the blind Gloucester encounters Lear ("mad, crowned with wildflowers"). Edgar's comment is significant: "O thou side-piercing sight!" Earlier on the stage, the eyes of Gloucester have been extruded—a deed of brute cruelty, a deed about which Johnson says, "seems an act too horrid to be endured in dramatic exhibition, and such as must always compel the mind to relieve its distress by incredulity."[10] The most shocking scene is the one where the mad Lear comes holding the dead Cordelia in his arms. It is a scene that, by tradition, is too excruciating to witness, so that through Tate in 1681 an alternate version circumventing this scene was introduced. Cordelia remains alive and marries Edgar, a version which prevailed on the stage until 1838.[11]

According to Holloway a parallel exists between *King Lear* and the book of Job.[12] Every time we suppose that the measure of suffering has reached its height, and that the light will break through, the cup of suffering contains yet another, even more bitter cup to swallow.

Although Shakespeare provides no solution for the enigma of suffering—and the effect of *King Lear* is overwhelming—one must be on guard against a sentimental interpretation of the play. To be sure, the suffering of Lear, Gloucester, Edgar, Kent, and Cordelia is suffering on a large scale. The *never, never, never, never* litany of Lear with the dead Cordelia in his arms is heart-rending. Death is a fearsome guest who has snatched the good Cordelia with his claws just at the moment where she is to about to be rehabilitated. The play lends its own weight to suffering and prevents any simple or easy solution.

10. Johnson, *The Plays of Shakespeare*, 121.

11. In an older version, *King Leir*, (the date is uncertain, c. 1594) this bloody conclusion is omitted. This could well be a discovery of Shakespeare himself.

12. In "The Story of the Night," cited by Jay L. Halio in the version of *King Lear* from *The New Cambridge Shakespeare*, 12.

All this is not to deny that certain voices have other things to say. These voices can also be heard throughout *King Lear*. One of them is that the men bring suffering on their own heads. This can certainly be said in the case of either Lear or Gloucester, although from the spectator's point of view the relationship between the punishment and the sin is not always proportionate. Edgar links Gloucester's adultery to his blindness:

> The gods are just, and of our pleasant vices
> Make instruments to plague us.
> The dark and vicious place where thee he got
> Cost him his eyes (5.3.168ff.).

Gloucester has fathered a son in a forbidden and dubious way, and the deleterious consequences are beginning to appear. Although to modern readers this may initially seem awfully disgusting, for Shakespeare and his society this infraction was taken very seriously. Gloucester's problems are seen as retribution, and one does not get very far in understanding the tragedies if one does not make this connection. Edgar, though, makes this statement not in the tone of a chilly reprisal. He is appalled at the brute blinding of Gloucester and grieves over the act. What happens, actually, is that Gloucester turns on and indicts himself as the perpetrator more than that there is a mechanical scheme of cause and effect. As in *Macbeth* the word brought to Macduff that his wife and children have been murdered, he responds, "Sinful Macduff, / They were all struck for thee. Naught that I am, / Not for their own demerits, but for mine, / Fell slaughter on their souls. Heaven rest them now!" (4.3.223ff.).[13] Suffering may induce introspection. It does not explain the suffering, but it is a mirror in which the victim learns to see himself as a transgressor.

All this is not intended to mean that behind every instance of suffering a moral trespass has to be detected. Some wrongly hold to the rigid idea that every person in the plays of Shakespeare deserves the death sentence. In such a worldview "it is but heading and hanging" (*Measure for Measure* 2.1.233). There are other voices worthy to be listened to.

Edgar provides such another voice. He is the one who prevents Gloucester from self-destruction. After all that he has endured, his father wishes to plunge off the cliffs of Dover:

> If I could bear it longer and not fall
> To quarrel with your great opposeless wills,

13. Dutch translation.

My snuff and loathed part of nature should
Burn itself out (4.6.37ff.).[14]

Because he can no longer embrace life, he will make an end of it. This question is a serious one: Why is a person willing to torment himself by lengthening out his days to their end? In the words of Edgar himself,

> . . . O, our lives' sweetness,
> That we the pain of death would hourly die
> Rather than die at once! (5.3.183ff.).

The sweetness of life usually prompts us to hold fast on to life, unless the bitterness becomes unbearable. And then? Even then one must sustain his will to live. He can perhaps discover no meaning in suffering, but his tenacity provides at least some moral strength. Edgar says to his father: "Bear free and patient thoughts" (4.6.79). "Free" here means innocent, not perturbed by troublesome thoughts; "patient" means here resolve, endurance. Later Edgar adds to this:

> What, in ill thoughts again? Men must endure
> Their going hence even as their coming hither.
> Ripeness is all. Come on (5.2.9ff.).

"Ripeness is all" parallels "the readiness is all" of *Hamlet* (5.2.195).[15] By these words he refers to a person's attitude; he should not be occupied with the question of when he is going to die and certainly not with the hour of his death, but he or she should ask how he would face the hour of his departure. Ripeness before death—that is to say, be ready for death. Ultimately it is about your condition, how you have lived your life. A person needs therefore to fend off "ill thoughts." It is a form of resignation which does not imply displaying an insensitivity towards one's lot, but will relieve the weight of this portentous moment. The moral questions are more significant than the questions of fortune.

And now a related comment from Edgar, one which refers to his own suffering. He says to Gloucester, who has asked his son where he is (Edgar is at the moment once again in another disguise):

> A most poor man, made tame to fortune's blows
> Who by the art of known and feeling sorrows
> Am pregnant to good pity (4.6.217ff.).

14. Dutch translation.
15. See. Foakes in his commentary on *King Lear*, 363ff.

"Pregnant to good pity:" I will comment on that a bit later on. But here I need to underscore that the highest virtue, *compassion*, gets born in suffering. Suffering of another or of oneself can teach one the quality of mercy. Not everything has been said with this answer, but the essence has been said. It is difficult in modern times to take these questions seriously, while fending off another's attempt to interpret such an effort ironically. Suffering for the modern sensibility is especially meaningless. The frameworks of reference have disappeared, and because of that, suffering is regarded as a brute force. Attempts to discern meaning are taken as insults. Opposed to all that is the choir of voices we find in Shakespeare's plays. True, they give no ultimate solution. Sometimes suffering blunts the person. The "exeunt with a dead march" at the end of *King Lear* calls only for silence. Listen to the voice of Gloucester:

> As flies to wanton boys are we to th' gods
> They kill us for their sport (4.1.38ff.).

Not a few see these last words as the quintessence of Shakespeare's view of life, but that is equally beside the mark, as is the dictum of Macbeth: "Life's but a walking shadow." The poet has permitted a whole choir of voices a hearing. But opposed to the bitter comment of Gloucester stands the shout of Albany when he learns that Cornwall has been killed by his own slave: "This shows you are above / you justicers" (4.2.79), and that of Edgar: "The gods are just" (5.3.168). We do not get an unequivocal vision. But no one who has once heard the five "never's" of Lear will arrive at any trivial answers.

Pilgrimage

Suffering—massive and dominating though it is—is not the only theme of *King Lear*. Both Lear and Gloucester undergo significant development. Much of the depth of this tragedy lies in the tracing of this development. Both are fallen fathers, and both have a laborious journey to achieve the necessary new insights. Seen in this light, *King Lear* can be interpreted as a pilgrimage of two sinners who arrive at a deeper understanding of themselves. There is no streamlined spiritual pilgrimage. It would be better to say there are moments of new insight. In Lear's case these flashes of insight sometimes break through the mist of his insanity, fighting against his self-pity and thoughts of revenge.

When Lear is confronted with the hard-heartedness of his daughters, his first reaction is to curse. It can be expected that a man who pushes Cordelia away from himself because she does not wish to join her sisters in their excessive flattery—that such a man will hardly be able to endure it when the other two daughters want to rob him of the last remnants of his kingship, treat him as old man, and want to lock him in a rest home for elderly people. The curses fill the air. And when Lear enters into the stormy night (because through the combined actions of Goneril, Regan, and Cornwall, his contingent of knights is denied shelter), then his damnations are as powerful as the storm. These curses extend to all that lives. He immediately, in the first explosion of his emotions, implores the elements to all at once make an end to the whole of reality:

> . . . And thou, all-shaking thunder,
> Strike flat the thick rotundity o'the world,
> Crack nature's mouths, all germens spill at once
> That make ingrateful man! (3.2.6ff.).[16]

This is the language of Macbeth when, in despair over his failures, he would prefer to destroy the whole of creation. Lear perceives reality through the magnifying glass of his own fate and wishes to let everything perish. Let the lightning strike with heavy mauls as the final judgment shatters the world to its foundations. The "angry ape" (*Measure for Measure*) cries out for the destruction of the world where his own ego endures suffering. These reactions towards personal calamity, though accompanied by deep pathos, indicate that Lear at that point has made not even a step towards self-knowledge.

Lear's resentment turns against mankind and, in a later phase, especially against women. In scene 4:6 he speaks the voice of cynicism. Lear shows kinship with Hamlet in this. Behind the façade of righteousness, injustice is hidden; behind morality, lusts play their filthy games. In place of condemning the whole show, Lear arrives at the still cynical conclusion: "None does offend, none." All morality is a sham that eliminates even the possibility of transgression. Lear has established his position on courtesy and servitude, expressions of praise and love to which he thought himself entitled. Now this balloon has been pricked; nothing rimes, and custom and morality are seen to have been merely a great show. One can hardly call this a path to deeper insight; rather, it is a matter of wounded

---

16. Dutch translation.

self-love. In these grotesque outbursts, Shakespeare has placed a mirror in which the spectator can recognize his own image. What is more universal than such wounded self-love?

Besides this cynicism comes predictable self-pity. Lear feels himself the victim of ingratitude, even though he had given everything over to his daughters: "I am a man, more sinned against than sinning" (3.2.59). But that is just the question. He has first shoved Cordelia out the door, deprived her of her promised inheritance, along with more or less a death sentence in place, and thereafter he is himself banished to the outdoors. While there is surely a difference of degree between offended vanity and heartless malice, still the language Lear has hurled against his own daughter is outrageous, and this also, like a boomerang, turns to rest on his own head. His self-pity is, then, also suspicious. Consider Lear's act of conducting a mock trial in which he sets himself up in the seat of the judge and simulates a trial in which Goneril and Regan are brought before him for judgment (scene 3:6, but it appears only in the Quarto text). This scene makes clear that Lear is still victim and does not understand that he himself sits in the complainer's bench. In this Lear has manifold companions.

But here and there another Lear makes an appearance. An early indication of this occurs the moment when he encounters "his poor fool" suffering from the cold (3.2.68ff.). For the first time Lear sees the lot of another. This insight gets reinforced later when Lear realizes that what he is now undergoing is what numerous outcasts experience daily—folk who cannot protect themselves from the night and the roar of the storm.

> Poor naked wretches, wheresoe'er you are
> That bide the pelting of this pitiless storm,
> How shall your houseless heads and unfed sides,
> Your looped and windowed raggedness defend you
> From seasons such as these? O, I have ta'en
> Too little care of this. Take physic, pomp,
> Expose thyself to feel what wretches feel,
> That thou mayst shake the superflux to them
> And show the heavens more just (3.4.28ff.).[17]

This is an insight of enormous importance. At the beginning of the play Lear views the map of his kingdom with great pleasure. Yet, for all

---

17. Dutch translation.

the expanse of that kingdom, his world has been a limited one. He has been ignorant of the lives of countless of his subjects. "O, I have ta'en / too little care of this." His "pomp" has blinded him. As your standing and well-being increase and your own security improves, the danger arises that whole segments of reality vanish from your field of vision. It is while Lear is dealing with the uncontrolled violence of the storm that these realities finally come crashing through to him. Wretches dwell in those regions—those who raise appeals for help. They have nothing, the others have too much. The excess, the *superflux*, is there to be distributed. Wealth is by itself not a curse, provided that it does not become a barrier to what man can accomplish through sharing.

Debora K. Shuger has demonstrated convincingly that Lear's words find their source in traditional Christian social ethics as they were developed during the patristic period and the Middle Ages.[18] Her words are worthy of citation: "Hence . . . Lear's prayer does not voice subversive heterodoxies—whether popular or humanist—but the social teachings of the medieval church. In his painful epiphany, the pagan king for a moment grasps the nature of Christian *caritas*."[19]

Remarkable, too, is Lear's "and show the heavens more just." *Caritas* is the form in which righteousness from the heavens manifests itself. Righteousness does not reflect itself in the first place in a balanced system of rights but in spontaneous deeds of kindness. On the other hand, those who withhold from the poor what they are entitled to, "they will be enraged and will curse their king and their God . . ." (Isa 8:21).

The insight which is breaking through in Lear is, therefore, directly related to *caritas*, or compassion. Pity and love are the virtues central to our lives. It is exactly against the background of the dark tragedies that these virtues shine in all their luster. Men are human precisely when they show compassion to the weak and whenever they show generosity with an unselfish love. Whether such compassion from a worldly point of view is successful is of lesser importance. Lear's insight advances when he is confronted with Cordelia. It is the power of Cordelia's love—a love that she does not owe him—that brings Lear to this confession:

18. Shuger, "Subversive Fathers and Suffering Subjects: Shakespeare and Christianity," in Hamilton and Strier, *Religion, Literature, and Politics in Post-Reformation England, 1540-1688*, 46–49.

19. Ibid., 53.

> . . . Pray, do not mock me:
> I am a very foolish, fond old man,
> Fourscore and upward,
> Not an hour more nor less;
> and to deal plainly,
> I fear I am not in my perfect mind (4.7.60ff.).

And more later:

> You must bear with me. Pray you now, forget
> And forgive. I am old and foolish (4.7.83ff.).

Cordelia is the banished daughter who has returned. The words of Lear reflect the words of the prodigal son who returns to his father and says, "Father, I have sinned against you and heaven and am no longer worthy to be called your son" (Luke 15:21). In one way or another, Lear is dependent on the actions of Cordelia for his self-knowledge. Before this he was not able to shed his self-pity and desire for revenge. The road towards self-knowledge is a narrow path. In spite of all the pleasant words, it is difficult for him to move on, imprisoned as he is in his own world. That world must be broken open through a sacrificial deed and unearned grace. As Lear wanders in his hell, he is met by this heavenly spirit, Cordelia. By her banishment the key to Lear's self-knowledge has been placed in the hands of the exiled. So weak is the strength of a tyrant that he is dependent on his banished daughter for his salvation.

The notion that the ideal of self-knowledge can be won in a silent corner of the world is false. Only in the turbulence of life, and in the wake of a deed of compassion, can one gain self-knowledge. Simply stated, only through a deed of uninhibited love can a person become truly himself. In our fallen world the only hope we have is one in which someone is shown true love and thereupon offers himself as a living sacrifice. That proves once again the pivotal role that love plays in the value-rich world of Shakespeare.

The Mentor

In another way, all this applies as well to Gloucester. His path to development I will pass over here. In many important ways it parallels that of Lear. But I wish to bring to the attention of the reader the role of Edgar. He is probably the most enigmatic figure of *King Lear*. He initially acts as a tame sheep displaced by his brother Edmund. Obviously this has to be accepted without much ado as the starting point for the following necessary actions of Edgar. He next adopts the disguise of "poor Tom," a role which he plays with great fervor. This play within a play is an amazing proof of Shakespeare's knowledge. The role of poor Tom is so robust that he in fact outdoes his role.[20]

Edgar plays this major role in order to serve as a guide to Glouces-ter. Again, he is the banished son who eventually must lead his father on his pilgrimage. He prevents Gloucester from committing suicide and mentors him on his path of suffering. He is "a blessing in disguise." He interacts with him directly, disguised as a madman and, later, in an ap-parently accidental encounter, in order to bring Gloucester a few steps further on his way. This Edgar is "pregnant to good pity," though he has been threatened with death by his father. He reasons with him against suicide and then shields him from an attempt by the lackey Oswald who intended to plot against him. He presents himself as a man who "Became his guide, / Led him, begged for him, saved him from despair" (5.3.189). It is puzzling why Edgar maintains his disguise so long. In fact, he regrets it himself: "Never—O fault!—revealed myself to him" (5.3.191). He does so finally, at the end; Gloucester, however, cannot bear the shock, and his heart gives out.

As already noted, the figure of Edgar is ambiguous. Granville-Barker describes him as "a Christian gentleman in a pagan play."[21] Negative char-acterizations, in my opinion, are not appropriate. The Folio version of 1623 possibly suggests that Edgar will be elevated to royal dignity. The banished son, the crazy man, the anonymous man then becomes the crowned king, who will reign along with Albany. It may be rightly said that Edgar is the most visible character in the whole play.

Edgar and Cordelia fulfill their saving functions through uncalculat-ing love—love they were not obliged to offer. The guide who really leads us to life does so out of *pity*. Once more, it appears that the world of the fallen fathers can be transformed only through the power of uncalculating

---

20. The fool is masterly in his cynical observations about Lear's decision to divide his kingdom, especially between two daughters who will eviscerate him. His witty observa-tions are amusing but accomplish little. "Poor Tom's" madness is a grade or two worse; he descends to deeper regions and does reach Lear.

21. Foakes, *King Lear*, 47.

love. That is the concealed source from which the fallen people become regenerated.

Cordelia

From what has already been said, the role of Cordelia is crucial. In spite of the fact that she appears on the stage only a short while and says little, she is the hidden pivot on which the play turns. Although I am hesitant, as I state in my introduction, to read Shakespeare allegorically, I am disposed to say that Cordelia points to Christ. She is an example of a post-figure in the sense that Balthasar defines the term. That is to say, glimmers of Christ radiate from Cordelia. In such a culture as the Elizabethan, strongly shaped by Christianity, such an inference is a reasonable one. This post-figure can also reflect light back on the figure. In the relationship between figure to post-figure, we speak of a "reincarnation." Cordelia calls up the power of a Christ-figure—though not in the context of the Bible.

This transparency thrusts itself upon us. At the beginning she is rejected by Lear. She is a "little seeming substance" (1.1.199). In Lear's eyes, she is less than nothing, and he believes he will not miss her. As the form of his curse has made clear, Lear appeals to the sun, Hecate, and the moving of the heavenly bodies, "from whom we do exist and cease to be" (1.1.113). This is paganism. This reference is natural, since it is necessary for the play to be set in a pagan context. However, people who possess "Christian ears" will also recognize the folly of paganism in these imprecations. Cordelia is sent into exile as the "new adopted to our hate / dowered with our curse" (1.1.196). Lear had expected to find repose in her "kind nursery," but now he rejects her as an enemy.

This rejection of Cordelia, in whom only truth and love exist—a love, however, that does not flatter or look with a calculating eye to her future—moves her into the pale of Christ himself. The French king well sees her worth. He sees in her the true bride:

> Fairest Cordelia, that art most rich being poor,
> Most choice forsaken, and most loved, despised,
> Thee and thy virtues here I seize upon (1.1.252ff.).

This judgment of France has a strong biblical ring to it. One thinks of such texts as "Jesus Christ . . . though he was rich, yet for your sakes he became poor, that ye through his poverty might be rich" (2 Cor 8:9).

Again, "He was despised, rejected of men" (Isa 53:3), and "My God, my God, why hast thou forsaken me?" (Ps 22:1).[22] It is a remarkable act for France to choose Cordelia—even more so now that she has been deprived of everything. Yet, she is still a prize, so that "not all the dukes of the waterish Burgundy / can buy this unprized precious maid of me (1:1:260ff.). She is beyond price. Here the voice of love rings out in its purest form.[23] Cordelia is banished by her father, but when she hears how her sisters are abusing him and how they have shoved him outdoors and locked him out, she decides that she must take passage and rescue him. Lear, singing loudly and with a crown of wildflowers in his hair, encounters a gentleman who declares to Lear:

> ... Thou hast a daughter
> Who redeems nature from the general curse
> Which twain have brought her to (4.6.201ff.).

The *twain* clearly refers to Goneril and Regan, but it is just as obvious that the two sisters do not exhaust this reference. Surely, the "general curse" applies not only to what the two sisters have done to Lear. The text points emphatically as well to a primeval history. The term *twain* actually points to Adam and Eve, who brought the "general curse" on successive generations. Here the actual history establishes a strong connection with the rich biblical background. Lear is the man who has come under the curse which has been brought into the world through the initial transgression. He is a deplorable figure who, while cursing himself all the time, lives under "the general curse." But here comes a daughter, who redeems man from the universal curse: Cordelia. This Cordelia becomes by this a post-figuration of Christ:

The saving character of Cordelia becomes clear when, just before Lear awakes from a deep sleep, she begs:

> O my dear father, restoration hang
> Thy medicine on my lips, and let this kiss

22. Shakespeare made use for *King Lear* of the new edition of the 1599 Geneva Bible (first printed in 1560), which included an abbreviated commentary on the apocalypse by a certain Junius (Francois de Jon); Shakespeare must surely have known this piece. David Daniell observes: "The play's imagery of cracking thunder, catastrophic earthquakes, wrathful dragons, prince of darkness, black angel, monsters of the deep, and much else is steeped in that book of the Bible" ("Reading the Bible" in Kastan, *A Companion to Shakespeare*, 170).

23. Cf. "unto you . . . which believe he is precious" (1 Pet 2:7).

Repair those violent harms that my two sisters
Have in thy reverence made (4.7.26ff.).

"Restoration," just as "redeem," is a word fraught with deep theological meaning. Cordelia wishes to heal her father with a kiss. The kiss is an act with a mystical meaning, as can be seen in the Song of Solomon 1:2, "Let him kiss me with the kisses of his mouth," which has become popular in the allegorical tradition of the interpretation of this text.[24] Another text is Psalm 45:2, where the messianic king says, "Grace is poured into thy lips." The reference to Christ becomes even more obvious through Cordelia herself, when, imprisoned and waiting with Lear to learn their dark fate, she comforts him with these words:

. . . We are not the first
Who with best meaning have incurred the worst.
For thee, oppressed king, I am cast down,
Myself could else outfrown false fortune's frown (5.3:3ff.)

It was not "blown ambition," but "dear, dear love" which has prompted Cordelia to beg permission from the French king to go to her father. She lives in France as queen, but she gives up her position for Lear and the worst possible punishment. For his sake she is "cast down," beaten down, imprisoned, in order, so it will appear, to be hanged as well. Lear acknowledges the magnanimity of her self-sacrifice:

Upon such sacrifices, my Cordelia,
The gods themselves throw incense (5.3.20ff.).

The "sacrifice" has implications beyond what the two of them realize at this moment. Cordelia is hanged. This shocking outcome, as noted earlier, is too horrible for many. In my opinion, this episode can be understood only in the "tragedy of the cross." There is within the Christian framework room for the tragic. The "My God, my God, why have you forsaken me?" points to the mystery of "God abandoned by God." This is more than an episode that in the light of the resurrection of Christ must be interpreted as a passing shadow. It is in the very scream emanating from the abandoned Christ that the negativity of existence is pressing together. The tear which runs through all of creation hits the Son of God and through him reaches God himself. In the Christian interpretation of

24. See, for example, the sermon of Bernard of Clairvaux, "Hij kusse mij met de kus van zijn mond."

such matters, tragedy is located at this point. But death here, however, assumes the character of a sacrifice, from where the fragrance of incense emanates. On the reverse is the text of the resurrection. This other side Shakespeare projects for us in his last plays. Tragedy has a proper place in God's redemptive history, but it does not have the last word. Tragedy as the last word excludes healing and reconciliation. But then the tragic dissolves into itself; it lacks a way out to meaning. It's the tragedy of meaninglessness in the figure of a mute and beaten-down human being that harks back to the idea that reality exposes an irresolvable inner contradiction.

Whenever *King Lear* is interpreted in such a way, it is the postmodern world view that is being projected, one which Shakespeare's antecedents and times would find strange. The death of Cordelia is a hard ending. But it is just because Cordelia is a Christ figure that we must speak against any sentimental notion. The night of Cordelia's death is reminiscent of the night of the cross. It finds an echo in the "Wir setzen uns mit Tranen nieder" with which Bach's *St. Matthew's Passion* ends. (We set ourselves down, with tears.) It awaits the first notes of the *Easter Oratorio*.

The conclusion of *King Lear*, in which an innocent Cordelia dies, exerts a powerful impact on the spectator. The stony hearts which we witness in the conflict between evil in its various guises (Edmund, Goneril, and Regan, and, in a different way, Lear) is set against the sacrifice of Cordelia and is also the occasion of her sacrifice. This is the extreme to which the rent in reality goes. Is it possible for one to see a "tua res agitur" (this is for you, too) in all this? Only a superficial public will not recognize this. It is another question whether a public would be inclined to see in the sacrifice of Cordelia a sign of an ultimate sacrifice that, despite all its negativity, opens the way to salvation and reconciliation. Or is this the real tragedy—that people no longer feel compelled to draw this conclusion?

7

The Tempest

THE TEMPEST IS LIKELY the last play that Shakespeare wrote independently. *Henry VIII* and *Two Noble Kinsmen* followed, but these were co-authored. *The Tempest* is also the last in a series of four plays that constitute a group known as tragi-comedies or romances. The other three plays are *Pericles*, *Cymbeline*, and *The Winter's Tale*.

The tragi-comedy genre is a category that originated in Italy about 1610 and became popular in England, especially through the efforts of the dramatists Beaumont and Fletcher.[1] According to their definition, a tragi-comedy is so designated not because of the pleasure of murder but because no death occurs. This feature is enough to prevent it from being a tragedy, although some of the plays get close to it, that, in turn, makes it less likely to be considered a comedy. This definition does not apply to 100 percent of Shakespeare's plays because Shakespeare's tragi-comedies are not altogether without deaths. Still, the definition is useful. The chief characters undergo great traumas, but they do not perish; on the contrary, they undergo renewal.

It is worthy of note that Shakespeare's tragedies, which have rightly become famous and are ranked high in the domain of world literature, are not his final words. That distinction is reserved for the tragi-comedies. This fact is enough to raise the question about whether one may infer from Shakespeare's achievement that his imagination inclined towards a tragic vision of life. Setting aside the question of whether or not Shakespeare's tragedies mirror a tragic vision of his own life, we must note a related fact suggesting the opposite—namely, that Shakespeare did not stay with the tragic genre. We can say with greater justice that the tragi-comedies may

---

1. General agreement prevails that Shakespeare co-authored *Henry VIII* with Fletcher.

be considered as the genre in which Shakespeare expressed his final and, at the same time, his deepest thought.[2] This is clearly suggested by the title of G. Wilson Knight's *The Crown of Life*, which is about Shakespeare's last plays.

Along the same line, let me cite still another series discussed by G. Wilson Knight. He has assigned descriptive titles to Shakespeare's plays. He arranges the last three groups of Shakespeare plays in a line, consisting of a trio: the problem plays, the tragedies, and the tragi-comedies. He asks himself on which model this series is based, assuming that Shakespeare did not follow this pattern accidentally (though he possibly was not wholly aware of this). Knight then refers to a Biblical analogy, the temptation of Jesus in the wilderness (problem plays); his tragic office and death (tragedies); and his resurrection from the dead (tragi-comedies).[3] According to Knight, these three categories of Shakespeare's work must be interpreted as analogies from an original. Indeed, these analogies have their own reality and are not allegories (as if the narratives were cloaks concealing some higher truth); at the same time they are based on an original context of meaning with which the plays sustain a deep resonance. The positive conclusion of the tragi-comedy is only through death, therefore suggesting a rising from death to life. That is no discovery of a creative writer but a religious belief that is inherent in a culture. Through the creative imagination of the playwright, such motifs are given a secular representation, whose transposition, however, is lost when the belief or the pointing to the belief is diminished or overlooked. Tragi-comedy has a metaphysical basis in the unique mission of Christ and, particularly, in his resurrection. As such, it is a "post-figuration" of Christ's resurrection (see my foreword).

The theme of "rising from the dead" plays an unmistakable role in the tragi-comedies. In *Pericles*, *The Winter's Tale*, and *Cymbeline* we see the sympathetic characters in the struggle against unfaithfulness, death, and ruin through which barriers are overcome, the loved ones who are lost are found again, and everyone seemingly dead comes to life again. That this pattern is linked with spiritual death and resurrection should not surprise anyone, in view of the fact that Shakespeare had already launched these themes in the "problem plays" and tragedies.

2. The Irish poet W. B. Yeats stated: "Shakespeare is always a writer of tragi-comedy" (*Essays*, 297).

3. Knight, *The Crown of Life*, 30ff.

The Narrative

The Tempest is a short play whose time frame lasts about three hours. It begins with a ship in peril, battered to and fro by a heavy storm. Eventually the ship breaks up. The passengers, however, unharmed, are tossed on to the beach of an island. It is an island that had been inhabited for many years by a certain Prospero and his daughter, Miranda. This Prospero is the former duke of Milan.

After the storm quiets down, Prospero relates to Miranda how twelve years ago, through the craftiness of his brother Antonio, he was divested of his dukedom. Antonio had breached the trust that Prospero had placed in him. Prospero had turned the government over to Antonio temporarily so that he could dedicate himself to his studies, including "secret studies"—that is, magic. Antonio, with the help of the king of Naples, Alonso, turned against Prospero and banished him. They forced him, together with his daughter, out to sea in a leaky vessel. Miraculously, the two managed to survive. They came upon an island, where Prospero has raised his daughter. He inhabited the island along with Ariel, an airy spirit, whom Prospero had liberated from the hands of the witch Sycorax. As thanks for this deliverance, Ariel has agreed to assist Prospero in his magical experiments. In addition to Ariel, Caliban, the son of Sycorax the witch, also lives on the island. In fact, he might make a claim to be the original inhabitant of the island. Prospero adopts him, and Miranda also expends great effort to teach him to become a civilized creature. When he tries to violate Miranda, Prospero makes him his slave.

By coincidence, the "drowned" persons who were washed up on the island have all been involved in Prospero's past history. In addition to Antonio and Alonso, already mentioned, we find Ferdinand, the son of Alonso, and Sebastian, his brother, along with certain lords and counselors, including Gonzalo, the jokester Trinculo, and the drunken butler Stephano. They were returning to Naples from an excursion in Tunisia in Algeria, where Claribel, the daughter of Alonso, had married the king of Tunis. It appears now that it was Prospero who had unleashed the storm; however, he did it not only through his own magical powers, but also through the cooperation of Ariel. The storm has a magical aura because all the passengers remain unhurt and because the ship, which had split, has been returned to land, sound and entire, complete with the crew, who were kept safe below the decks. After the tossed passengers are washed ashore, Alonso, Antonio, Sebastian, and certain lords find each other. Ferdinand remains apart. Later, Stephano and Trinculo find each other and form a group with the indigenous Caliban. Because the various groups wander about in different places, each member thinks himself to be one of the only survivors.

Prospero has aroused the storm in order to get the whole group into his power. He will now begin his project. Ferdinand, who is mourning the loss of his father, now meets Miranda, and it becomes a matter of love at first sight; the relationship ends in marriage. For the people of Alonso's group, Prospero devises a series of tests that they must meet. He will confront them with painful experiences and in so doing hopes to bring them to repent of the shameful deeds that they had perpetrated against him in the past. In the meantime the group of Stephano, instigated by Caliban, plot to kill Prospero—though their plot is unsuccessful.

Ultimately they all get to meet Prospero, where they learn and discover how everything happened. Alonso comes to regret his activities and restores the dukedom to Prospero. Antonio and Sebastian appear to remain hardened sinners. Miranda, as the wife of Ferdinand, becomes queen of Naples. Prospero vows to end his practice of magic and addresses the public in an epilogue.

Deep Sea Changes

The four tragi-comedies are grouped together through comparable thematic devices. In each, persons are separated from each other, but in wonderful ways they are also restored to each other. Other motifs come into play; punishment and repentance, forgiving and reconciliation play an important role. The climax of the play focuses primarily in the recognition of lost and supposedly dead loved ones. The most prominent example in this context is surely the moment when Pericles in that particular play recognizes his supposedly dead daughter and is reunited with her.[4]

In *The Tempest* the recognition, in this case, of a supposedly dead father by his son, plays a similar role. That episode is not the dominant one, although it is intimately involved with it. As for the primary motif, I refer to a scene in act 1.2. There we encounter Ferdinand, the son of the king of Naples, Alonso, on the beach. He is mourning the death of his

---

4. *Pericles*, 5.1.134–237. Inspired by this encounter, T. S. Eliot wrote his *Mariana*.

father. Now the invisible spirit, Ariel, appears, and the astonished Ferdinand hears the following words:

> Full fathom five thy father lies,
> Of his bones are coral made;
> Those are pearls that were his eyes,
> Nothing of him that doth fade
> But doth suffer a sea-change
> Into something rich and strange.
> Sea nymphs hourly ring his knell (1.2.397ff.).

This is a charming piece of poetry. The drowned king lies five fathom deep, at the bottom of the sea. He is certainly dead, because sea nymphs hourly ring his death knell. But this death is not the last word. The king does not perish, but undergoes "a sea change." Under water his bones are transformed into coral and his eyes into pearls. He becomes transformed into a being both rich and strange, so that it cannot be compared with anything else.

Obviously, the dead, through drowning, have achieved a new and richer existence. This change, however, could have come about only in water. The "full fathom five thy father lies" suggests the power of a definite judgment. Alonso has really disappeared below the water line, unreachable by human hands. He is there because of the storm which has delivered him up to the destructive waters. This storm is a judgment. It has been the means by which the passengers have been cut loose from their own world, along with all their certainties and supposed attainments.

The idea of reclamation by means of water is expressed as well in the explanation that Prospero provides through the unprecedented storm he has raised. He assures Miranda that no one has lost so much as a hair; on the contrary, their clothes are "fresher than before" (1.2.119). Life upon the island itself can be seen as an existence resulting from a transformation.

The renewal by water, however, has the function of a symbol. The person who lacks any trace of inner renewal, or shows no indication of willingness to undergo such renewal, will not even recognize the renewal of the garments, as seems to be case with Sebastian and Antonio. They also remain blind and deaf to the language that the storm has spoken. They are cynical idlers who misuse the moment of crisis of the usual certainties for their own advantage.

The fact that Alonso's "drowned" body has undergone a sea change points to a spiritual rebirth. The first step lies in the acknowledgment of the judgment that the storm has announced and also the acceptance of the "downfall" which it implies. Alonso is wholly convinced when he says that he heard the storm speak:

> ... O, it is monstrous, monstrous!
> Methought the billows spoke and told me
> The winds did sing it to me, and the thunder-
> The deep and dreadful organpipe—pronounced
> The name of Prosper. It did bass my trespass.
> Therefore my son I' th' ooze is bedded, and
> I'll seek him deeper than e'er plummet sounded
> And with him there lie mudded (3.3.95ff.).[5]

When Alonso speaks these words, he has along with his group witnessed the strange image of a table prepared for dinner but which, however, at the moment they wish to enjoy the food, is withdrawn, "in thunder and lightning." This vividly recalls "the thunder and lightning" at the beginning of the play. These events now begin to get Alonso's serious attention. He now understands the language of the storm—the surging waves, the wind, and the thunder that pronounced the name of Prospero—and "bass his trespass." He knows his son is embedded at the bottom of the sea, and there he intends to seek him and join him in the muddy bottom. It is in this way that the prophecy of Ariel is being fulfilled in Alonso's life.

That the storm itself and the vanishing banquet constitute a judgment becomes clear from Ariel's announcement of it. Ariel says in plain-spoken language that his son has perished and that, he, Alonso, will undergo "ling'ring perdition"—worse than a one-time death ever could be. This is language from hell, and this continuing damnation has reference to Alonso and his ways. There is but one way out. That way does not consist in a direct transposition in paradisal circumstances. The royal banquet is removed, and the island is described at that moment as "most desolate." The true way is "Nothing but heart's sorrow / And a clear life ensuing" (3.3.81ff.).

This is the actual deep sea change about which Ariel spoke. Alonso actually experiences it. That appears at the end. There he meets Prospero,

---

5. Plaisier here offers the quotation in Dutch.

who informs him that both his daughter and Alonso's son have perished. Alonso would be willing himself in order to retrieve both of them (so as to make them king and queen of Naples) to bury himself "in that oozy bed" (5.1.151) at the bottom of the sea. He uses the same words that he had used earlier, as cited above. Whereas Alonso initially arranged for the death of Prospero and his daughter, he is now prepared to die in order to rescue his son and Prospero's daughter. Where he first deprived a daughter of her queenly dignity (although he was more an accomplice than a perpetrator), he would now bequeath her a kingdom at the cost of his own life. This is a profound change in Alonso, which brings him into the kingdom of the forgiven. It is Prospero who must do the forgiving. I will return to this matter. At this point it is important to note that the whole series of disasters which Alonso has experienced is being described as "not natural," but miraculous. As the crew of the ship, uninjured, appears, they comment:

> These are not natural events; they strengthen
> From strange to stranger (227ff.).

And a little later:

> This is as strange a maze as e'er men trod,
> And there is in this business more than nature
> Was ever conduct of. Some oracle
> Must rectify our knowledge (242ff.).

"Strange"—that is more than only miraculous. These words, "this is as strange a maze as e'er men trod," harks back to the "something rich and strange" from "the deep sea change." The wonder of the external happenings are mirrored in the wonder of the inner transformation. And this is all more than only superficial, sly-as-a-fox changes. The earlier song of Ariel points to the sacrament of baptism. All this involves the renewal of the person, upon whom grace has been efficacious. What is also implied is that "some oracle" must report the final result. That oracle can be found in a different book. The island and its magical aura, in which one and another has been behaving, constitutes the setting which the wonder of the deep sea change makes possible. It is a meaningful and astonishing mirror of the mystery of baptism: new life through death, the "magic immersion" in which the baptized child loses its life and receives it back again and, thus, is united with the dead and resurrected Christ.

Spiritual Obduracy

Alonso undergoes a sea change, but Antonio and Sebastian, who also belong to this group, do not follow suit. For them, the trial of the storm followed by the experience of being set on the island does not lead to self-appraisal. Antonio, as the brother of Prospero, in fact the chief offender, turns out to be a cynical joker. The disruption of the normal order is for him a chance to extend his power and, as the occasion arises, urges Sebastian, the brother of Alonso, to murder the latter. Through magical intervention, Alonso falls into a deep sleep. Because he originally speaks in veiled terms, Sebastian is slow in apprehending what Antonio has in mind. As it begins to dawn on him, he says:

> . . . I remember
> You did supplant your brother Prospero.
> Antonio: True:
> And look how well my garments sit upon me
> Much feater than before (2.1.271ff.).

Antonio attributes the renewal of his clothes to his own actions. They sit on him better after the "murder" than before. Thus, he closes off the road to remorse. Sebastian, ill at ease concerning the murder, raises the question of one's conscience. Antonio cynically answers that he cannot find "this deity" in his heart. Even should twenty consciences bar the way between him and the kingdom of Milan, they would "melt before they molest." Antonio lacks a conscience. Still, no real tension occurs. Antonio is too insignificant and trivial a man for a real tension to occur. He misses the format from which he could develop into a tragic figure. The play refuses to revolve around this turning point. Antonio, however, remains with us somewhat like a fishbone in the throat. The forgiveness which Prospero extends to him at the closing has no effect on the evildoer. In the absence of any sign of penitence, the forgiveness is not genuine or heartfelt, and Prospero cannot get the word "brother" past his lips.

The Tempest does not have an unqualified "happy ending." Forgiving and reconciliation are not in the hearts of those who, through the agency of "the tempest," refuse to join the new community. In that respect The Tempest differs from The Winter's Tale. In that play King Leontes, the most guilty, expresses undeniable contrition and, though having lost his daughter and wife through his fault, they are restored to him as if from death. But in The Tempest the reader or spectator is confronted with the obstinacy of human nature. It does not rise to the level of a tragedy, however. Rather, Sebastian and Antonio are lowered to the status of nonpersons. They do not share in the joy of the new community; they do not undergo "a sea change" and therefore become marginalized and simply vanish as the play ends. And the rest is silence. Does that perhaps leave a bitter aftertaste—more than is the case with such scoundrels as Edmund, Iago, and Macbeth? Are not all these insignificant, cynical folk who, in the dark, strike blows, slippery as eels, not capable of comprehending the greatest desires of the heart and stand uncomprehending before the great experiences of liberation and blessing—are not these characters who stick like a fishbone in the throat?

Low Characters

We see a coarser form of evil in the group Trinculo and Stephano. Stephano is a drunken butler and Trinculo is a jokester. They come upon Caliban. This character is complex, but in any case he is resentful and resigns himself only reluctantly to the authority of Prospero. When he is filled with alcohol he designates alcohol as "celestial liquor" and the donor of it as "a brave god" (2.2.115). He had claimed earlier that Prospero was a usurper ("This island's mine by Sycorax, my mother, which thou tak'st from me" (1.2.332), but now he is willing, literally, to kiss Trinculo's foot (2.2.149).

The group now determines, at the suggestion of Caliban, to go to Prospero's cave and to murder him in his sleep. Stephano will then become king of the island and Caliban his lowly servant. Trinculo tags along. Naturally, they will never arrive at this point. Ariel lures them through music into a stinking marsh. Stephano and Trinculo call to mind the scene of the famous Falstaff in *King Henry IV*. Falstaff is also the droll wag who, when inebriated, charms the public. It appears that ultimately these feckless characters cannot be salvaged. What Knight applies to another such character, Autoclytus in *The Winter's Tale*, also applies to these characters: "No one can accuse Shakespeare of lacking a sense of humor, but it is too often forgotten that his humor functions within the bounds of a persistent "high seriousness."[6] Whenever they give an indication of lust for and longing for power, these buffoons fall all over themselves and do

---

6. Knight, *The Crown of Life*, 113.

not come off either without scratches and bruises. By the way, compared with the petty characters Stephano and Trinculo, Falstaff comes off as a superior humorist, but even he ends as a self-extinguished star. Stephano and Trinculo are petty folk who dream great dreams. At the end of the play Stephano, a stinking mess and wearing stolen garments, appears before Prospero and must endure his taunt: "You'd be the king o' the isle, sirrah?" (5.1.288). Stephano has no answer. They stand, non-entities, invisible and insignificant. There is a world of butlers and buffoons. They smell bad, too.

Caliban

The above cannot be said about Caliban. He occupies too prominent a place in the play. This is not the place to elaborate on the varying interpretations of this aboriginal. Those who hold that the central theme of the play lies in the imperialism of "the new world" will describe him as the key character. I view this as an anachronistic interpretation (its starting point can be found in modern sensibility), and I therefore cannot view Caliban as the key figure. One would rather say this about Ariel, who is always closely involved in the execution of Prospero's project.

This is not to deny that Caliban remains an intriguing character. He does not belong in the category of the villain, as do Edmund or Iago. I would prefer to designate him as the image of natural man, the "heathen." He is the aboriginal who has been adopted by Prospero and is being initiated into his civilization. He has learned to speak its language and has, therefore, raised himself to a level higher than a mere primitive. Miranda has also contributed to this process:

> ... I pitied thee,
> Took pains to make thee speak, taught thee each hour
> One thing or other (1.2.354ff.).

Caliban, however, has fallen; has attempted to violate Miranda. That folly radically alters the situation. Now he falls under judgment. The question naturally arises whether this judgment is the just one and whether it is right for Prospero to supervise him by his rigid standards. Now Caliban is denigrated to the level of a slave. Thus Prospero and Miranda repudiate their own standards. One finds not a spark of compassion in Prospero. It is true in a way that differs from Caliban that Prospero is also a "heathen."

Caliban is suppressed. Every time he refuses to carry out orders, he is subjected to various punishments. What is even more disturbing is the devastating judgment which Prospero, but also Miranda, pronounces on Caliban:[7]

> ... But thy vile race
> (Though thou didst learn) had that in't which good natures
> Could not abide to be with (1.2.359ff.).

He is described as "an abhorred / slave which any print of goodness wilt not take" (1.2.352). Miranda confirms her prejudicial attitude by this demonization of Caliban. For his part, Caliban describes himself as disinherited. After all, he says,

> This island's mine by Sycorax, my mother,
> Which thou tak'st from me (1.2.332ff.).

Caliban is without perspective. He attempts in vain to shed his yoke. He will never miss an opportunity do so. He gets his chance when Stephano, the drunken butler, appears. He puts them up to murdering Prospero. Thus, he falls into a depraved company. Ironically enough, he accepts the rule of Stephano. Under the influence of liquor (also a product of a civilized Europe), Caliban even offers to kneel before him, kiss his foot, and "by the bottle" swear to become his subject. Now as his dream to shed off his yoke can become reality, he demeans himself, prompted by his drunkenness, to become the slave of a play king and a drunken god. In his mad frenzy he sings: "Freedom, high-day; high-day freedom, freedom high-day, freedom" (2.2.181). A little later the trio sings: "Thought is free" (3.2.123). This sort of freedom rests on weak knees (literally as well; see 3.2.6). Caliban is not prepared for freedom, and he degenerates into a slavery that is worse than the slavery from which he wishes to free himself. As was the case earlier with Jack Cade, it becomes clear that the rebellious spirit which defies proper authority always leads to a new form of slavery.

Still, Caliban is no mere sly scoundrel either. He jumps madly with joy when Stephano promises to murder Prospero. He is nature's child; he has both an eye and an ear for the beauties of the island. One of the most charming poetic passages comes from the mouth of Caliban:

7. Some editors assign this passage to Prospero, with some justification. See the Arden Shakespeare, third series, 135–6.

Be not afeard. The isle is full of noises,
Sounds and sweet airs that give delight and hurt not.
Sometimes a thousand twangling instruments[8]
Will hum about mine ears; and sometimes voices,
that if I then had waked after long sleep,
Will make me sleep again (3.2.135ff.).

Anyone who is not open to the beauties of this music fits the description of such a person in *The Merchant of Venice*; he is one who is "fit for treason, stratagems, and spoils" (5.1.85).

As already noted, things do not work out well for the trio, and Caliban finally realizes that he has been betting on the wrong horse. His last words, directed towards Prospero, reveal a new insight. As he receives Prospero's order to "trim handsomely" his (Prospero's) cell, he replies,

Ay, that I will; and I'll be wiser hereafter
And seek for grace. What a thrice-double ass
Was I to take this drunkard for a god,
And worship this dull fool! (5.1.295ff.).

The idea of freedom as Caliban had imagined it was a pipe dream. He will from now on "seek for grace." Does he capitulate only to avoid punishment? That appears to me a childish interpretation. Or does it open a way to achieve true humanity? Not through reading out of a book of manners, nor adopting a servant's obsequiousness, but it is through "grace" that there is a "hereafter" for Caliban. The play actually ends at this point. The future of Caliban remains open. Prospero will retire, and from that we might conclude that Caliban will now recover his freedom.

Prospero and Miranda push back, reminding Caliban of his origins as the son of Sycorax. Therefore it must be concluded that Prospero has failed in his attitude towards Caliban. Put even more directly: Caliban is a living, derivative image of Prospero himself. Prospero recognizes that self-image. He admits as much at the end of the play:

. . . This thing of darkness I
acknowledge mine (5.1.275).

Prospero has repelled Caliban and banished him from his magical kingdom. One who proceeds in this way does not realize that by so doing he denies his own dark nature. The so-called enlightened half can, in fact,

8. "tinkling" instruments.

take on the guise of tyranny. Prospero's acknowledgement that Caliban is his doing opens a way for him to achieve a wholly new personhood, clothed now with the rich robes of grace and forgiveness, the only womb for true humanity. That brings me to Prospero.

Prospero

Prospero is unmistakably the central figure of *The Tempest*. The storm and everything that follows in its wake is his "project." Although he may not have had a direct hand in nudging the ship with its passengers to his island, for the rest he is the stage manager for the events to which he has set his hand. To do this he uses his magical powers, for which he is actually dependent on Ariel. It is at the moment towards the end of the play where he sheds his mantel and abandons his books of magic, that he restores Ariel's freedom.

In the story itself, Prospero is not only the stage manager but also an actor. These two functions are intertwined. Prospero, for example acts towards Ferdinand and, later, those of the group, when they appear before his cave.

It is not easy to provide a coherent and satisfying account of Prospero. He is one who as duke of Milan dedicated himself to "liberal arts" (1.2.73) and "secret studies." His efforts involving the sciences went hand in hand with "the bettering of my mind" (1.2.90). Still, these studies estranged him from his political duties. It is right to fault him for this. Self-improvement, after all, was a project focused on Prospero himself. His "Machiavellian" serious-minded brother found it all too simple to use the free hand he was given, to take over Prospero's duties.

Prospero develops during the course of the play. He is knowledgeable concerning both nature and magic and the skill to practice them together. For that purpose he uses Ariel. This wonderful, attractive figure is a sort of embodiment of nature, with magical powers, poetry and music, "an airy spirit." On the other hand, there is his relationship with Caliban, as previously narrated.

Prospero is a strict master who in no way resembles the absentminded, learned man he was in Milan. He rules events with a strong hand; he steers the plot and commands both Ariel and Caliban. He discovers his limits: he cannot govern the inner life of others. He has no power over the heart of others.

Prospero is not immune from absorbing the ideals of the Renaissance. We see also in that a new fascination for nature—the typical combination of science and magic, the mythical and the folkloristic elements. The Renaissance sees humanity as manager over forces as well as gifts, a status that designates him the privileged center point of the universe.

In addition to being scientist and magician, Prospero is also the educator and colonizer. He has informed himself about the external world, with all of its fascination. This achievement summons in him the desire to wake civilization up. That this all or nothing supposed superiority leads also to a form of colonization and exploitation in *The Tempest* is abundantly clear. And Prospero is dependent for his luxurious life on a slave whom he orders to do the heavy work of tidying up his cell—and without any scruples about doing so. The Renaissance is the era which has promoted the motion of "the white man's burden."

Prospero's art must be mentioned as a third aspect of his identity. He enchants with music and devises diverse pageants. Ariel is the intermediary here as well. Through Ariel he creates virtual worlds and christens the island to become a setting for poetry and especially music. And thus now it is not going too far afield for us to see Prospero as a figure in whom Shakespeare had mirrored himself. He also, through the power of his poetic talent, has held the public in his grip. He has shaped one virtual world after another and has something in him of the magician. He is also one for whom each play has been a "project," firmly in the hand of the almighty stage director.

In the play *Faustus*, written by Marlowe, one of Shakespeare's contemporaries, we see how this power takes on an infernal bent. Faustus severs himself from the world of morality and religion and, thus, his knowledge becomes diabolic. This is surely not the case with Prospero. It was not, in any event, an idle resolve he harbored in Milan to improve himself. As he arouses the storm, he takes great care that no one is injured. And even when Miranda shows fear, he calms her down:

> . . . Be collected;
> No more amazement. Tell your piteous heart
> There's no harm done (1.2.13ff.).

Although he deals harshly with Ferdinand, and, to all appearances, unjustly, this finally appears to be probationary; he does this in order to test the authenticity of his love. His management of diverse characters is likewise masterly, but not per se unjust. The moral equilibrium of this magician, however, is unstable. As noted earlier, Caliban is the open question about Prospero: Where are you headed? How can Prospero be prevented, perhaps on the basis of his scientific and moral grounds, from gravitating towards the devil?

At the critical moment, however, Prospero receives a challenge. He needs to have sympathy towards his enemies. Speaking to Ariel, who more or less provokes him to this, he demonstrates the first glimmerings of compassion. He knows:

> Though with their high wrongs I am struck to th' quik
> Yet with my nobler reason 'gainst my fury
> Do I take part. The rarer action is
> In virtue than in vengeance. They being penitent
> The sole drift of my purpose doth extend
> Not a frown further (5.1.25ff.).[9]

Offering forgiveness is an active deed. To do so, Prospero must renounce his anger and overcome the urge to avenge. The virtue of forgiveness is a rare one, and really creates something new. This action lies on a different level from that of Prospero the stage director, who keeps a tight grip on the ropes of the play. To forgive, he has to overcome an inner obstacle. He decides to do so. He steps out of his role as judge and avenger and offers forgiveness.

But he does more. Prospero also finally yields his magical powers. He announces that to Ariel as well, in the last act: "But this rough magic / I here abjure (5.1.50). By "rough" the playwright intends to describe Prospero's magic as dubious, coarse, outrageous.

Once more will he produce music by his magical wand, after which he intends to break it:

> I'll break my staff,
> Bury it certain fathoms in the earth,
> And deeper than did ever plummet sound
> I'll drown my book (5.1.54ff.).

---

9. Dutch translation.

Magic wand, magic book, the instruments which have made him powerful—he will destroy and bury them. The metaphor of burying, so fundamental in *The Tempest*, is returning. The "certain fathoms" refers to the "full fathoms five" from Ariel's song, and the "plummet sound" to the "plummet sounded" in the confession of Alonso. The knowledge of magic possibly serves as a shield behind which true mankind can disappear. First it distracted Prospero from his "social function" as the ruling duke, and now they would make him out to be a semi-god incapable of communicating with others, only manipulating them as marionettes. He can acquire a new life only by presenting himself before his fellowmen as a dependent creature. This becomes crystal clear from the epilogue, which should be regarded as a definitive conclusion to the play. And it is here that the identification between Prospero and the playwright Shakespeare becomes clear. Both stand with empty hands before the public. What power they now have is "most faint" (epilogue, 3). They have no "spirits to enforce, art to enchant" any more (14). What does he now require?

> And my ending is despair,
> Unless I be relieved by prayer,
> Which pierces so that it assaults
> Mercy itself, and frees all faults.
> As you from crimes would pardoned be,
> Let your indulgence set me free (13ff.).

The apotheosis of the play shows a man who has learned forgiveness and who must now be forgiven and become freed through grace. That is why he asks for the prayers and the good will of the public. Is it also possible that this epilogue marks a conclusion to Shakespeare's work? He has foresworn the Faustian dream. He voluntarily lays aside his magical arts. This is an extremely important motif of the play. Nothing would prevent Prospero from maintaining his magical tools, and, thus the power to control his opponents—and, indeed, to remain absolute ruler on the island. He does not do any of these. He would then block the way to his own identity. He would then become the great manipulator, and his power would know no bounds. By breaking his staff and burying it and restoring Ariel's freedom, Prospero acquires his own freedom. Not that this reduces him to a wimpish impotence. He gets his dukedom back and will be obliged to serve it with honor, but he does surrender the island and foregoes his magical powers.

The fact is that Prospero had always been a dependent person. It is Gonzalo who had saved his life. And it is the power of providence which comes to Prospero's aid when he was banished to the island. Gonzalo points out the role of providence throughout the action—whose power supersedes that of man and who made it possible for the characters to find what they sought or what they needed:

> . . . and all of us ourselves,
> When no man was his own (5.1.212ff.).

In the final analysis *The Tempest* is about the question of identity. No one is himself—not Prospero lost in his studies, not Prospero as the mighty magician, nor the king, nor the prince, nor the perpetrator, nor the victim. The "self" is a gift from the gods, which is obtained through humility, grace, and forgiveness.

The great Renaissance poet William Shakespeare has summoned up his most powerful figure: Prospero. In him we find everything which modern man has acquired. Prospero is a fascinating figure and, in a certain sense, the flower of humanity. But he reaches his goal only when he knows where to let go and enter the kingdom where forgiveness, grace, and mercy reign. Through humiliation we are resurrected; through suffering we rise. The law that applies to the guilty also applies to good people if their goodness is not to develop into a hell worse than the hell of the villain.

Appendix I

Some Methodological Reflections Concerning the Theme "Theology and Literature"

A Division of Assets?

THIS STUDY PROCEEDS FROM the notion that theologians will find it rewarding to busy themselves in the study of authors such as Shakespeare. Speaking more generally, this essay is an experiment of interaction between two distinct territories—theology and literature. In my opinion, this interaction is a fruitful and necessary one for study, especially for the theologian.

But the life of the world takes little note of such a subject. The situation does, after all, have a cause, an origin. Literature in the Western world has all but completely detached itself from theology. Over many centuries of time the process of secularization has firmly established itself. Any reference to belief as an existential reality or to God as a living presence is not easy to find. The presuppositions of modern Western Europe culture is that reality is self-authenticating, and that attitude also gets reflected in its literature. This is frequently not a conscious assumption, but an unconscious disposition, one held by both author and reader. At the same time a resistance prevails against any outside influence that could rob literature of its autonomy. The author is forbidden to be a voice for any source other than literature, especially if that source claims authority from a source beyond the human. Literature is seen as an autonomous terrain and is not to be "demeaned" by being compelled to serve some higher goal.

All this is of a piece with the idea that literature is not to be reviewed by use of non-literary criteria, such as the moral or theological. These admonitions apply not only to the interpretation of contemporary literature but also to literature from the past. Any idea that in literary criticism any test of morality may be applied is regarded as a transgression of boundaries or a transposition of genres. Besides this, in modern literary criticism, there is, because of the taste of the age, the tendency to underexpose the moral and theological dimensions in a "secular" literature, also of literature in which modern presuppositions were not part of the shared world-and-life view.

On the other hand, it seems true as well that theology nowadays has little to do with literature. The actual occupation of theology with literature hardly exists, but for a few exceptions. One finds in The Netherlands scarcely any serious theological acknowledgment of literature either from the past or the present. Theologians prefer to stick to their own last. This has not always been the case. Among the ethics theologians—a movement in the nineteenth century—the boundaries were less narrowly defined.[1] J. H. Gunning and, later, Is. Van Dyk, frequently ventured on to the literary terrain.[2] Even in the more recent past this trait still achieved a following. One thinks of K. H. Miskotte and the numerous impressive books and publications about past and present literature that he has published.[3] He has had few followers. It seems that theology took up philosophy more seriously, and in more recent times it has busied itself more with sociology, psychology, and other social sciences. The older humanism, which included literary works, has always come off poorly, and "world literature" has never been included as part of a theological curriculum. The reason is probably that world literature in a theological curriculum would not lead to any tangible result, and theology as scientific discourse (which theology certainly is and ought to be) does not seem to harmonize with theology as a form of art that is literature.[4]

---

1. Alexander Vinet proved an important inspiration for this movement. Next to his theological and ethical publications, he occupied himself intensively with literary criticism. He wrote about French literature of the nineteenth century, among others, about Lamartine, Victor Hugo, Madame de Stael, and Chateaubriand.

2. We take notice of Gunning's studies about Dante (1870); Van Dijk wrote studies about (among others) Shakespeare and Ibsen's *Brand* (*Gezamenlijke Geschriften* I), George Eliot and Van Eeden's *Johannes Viator* (*Gezamenlijke Geschriften* III).

3. Miskotte, *Messiaans verlangen and other literuur—and cultuurkritische opstelllen*.

4. Rudolf Bohren had this to say: "Warum legen die Theologen unter viel Seufzen

The Bible

That a relationship exists between theology and literature is beyond doubt. The source book of theology, the Bible, is, of course, very much a literary book. It contains books and cycles of biblical narratives which can be regarded as great literature. One needs only to think about Genesis, Job, the Psalms, the chronicles of David and his successors, Isaiah, the evangelists, the book of Revelation. Each of these books has its own style, its own degree of narrative art, of imagination, of composition, that can be affirmed as literature. Moreover, the Bible is in its entirely a literary product, that can compare favorably with *The Iliad* and *Odyssey* of Homer. The Bible is, thus, surely a book that can be read from a literary point of view.[5] It can be analyzed in terms of linguistics, figures of speech, narrative technique, the use of images, symbols, and parables.

Beyond all this, the Bible has profoundly influenced the world of letters. Eric Auerbach has explained convincingly what is characteristic of the biblical style. He elaborated his findings about these characteristics and how the informative influence of this style has shaped European literature. He points to the realism of the Middle Ages and the Early Modern period, times in which an elevated style was not closed off from every day life, empirical perceptions, and realism; the low style in its turn could pick up the deepest eternal and high concerns.[6] In another study Auerbach points to the metaphorical character of the biblically-inspired literature in which events take on a heightened meaning when related to the central drama—the redemptive drama.[7] From another direction we hear Northrop Frye, who studied the stylistic characteristics of the Bible and proposed the thesis that the Bible has served as the great code of European literature, at least until the eighteenth century.[8] Biblical narrators and artists have at various times been greatly influenced, consciously or unconsciously, by the Bible.

grossen Wert darauf, im Haus der Wissenschaften zu wohnen? Warum gehen sie am Haus der Kunst vorbei?" (Why are the theologians, with heavy sighs, so eager to live in the house of science? Why do they bypass the house of art?) (*Geist und Gericht*, 180). Cf. also his *Dass Gott schön werde*.

5. Cf. Fokkelman and Wren, *De Bijbel literair*.

6. Auerbach, *Mimesis*, 78.

7. Auerbach, "Figura."

8. Frye, *The Great Code: The Bible and Literature*.

One of the goals of my study was to demonstrate that Shakespeare cannot be understood if one fails to take into account the influence of the Bible. Shakespeare wrote in a context in which the Bible had a very direct influence in shaping the lives of the people. The English Reformation especially was a movement that made the Bible available to the common people. One needs to be mindful, however, that an exclusive literary approach to the Bible annihilates the Bible. In the words of T. S. Eliot, "the Bible has had an influence upon English literature, *not* because it was regarded as literature but because it has been considered as the report of the Word of God. And the fact that men of letters now discuss it as 'literature' probably indicates the *end* of the Bible's literary influence."[9] The Bible has had a dramatic influence on literature, not as a literary book, but as a book of faith. This holds as well in the case of Shakespeare.

The "Christian" Period

Now and then the theologian is made to appear like a poor asylum-seeker who travels to the land of literature as to a foreign country. That is, perhaps, a neat comparison to today's situation, in which the theologian can better return to the land of his origins from which he came. This comparison in any event was not the case for major periods of European history. In the Middle Ages artists shared religious beliefs with others. It is not surprising that these beliefs continually make their presence felt in the artistic world, although there is a difference between religious and secular art. *The Divine Comedy* and *The Decameron* are, from that point of view, very different works. After the Middle Ages these shared religious assumptions changed only slightly, but though the world of religious branches multiplied (Reformed, Anabaptist), the secular world got the upper hand over religious art. In the next centuries the shared religious world-and-life-view begins to pale more and more, even though this view had not yet entirely disappeared in the nineteenth century. In our time this commonness has disappeared almost completely. As I mentioned earlier, imaginative writers and readers no longer write out of a religious consciousness, and writers no longer share a community of beliefs. Literature for many has taken the place of religion, and writers create their own world of truth and emotion. They mostly reflect the hidden assumptions of the spirit's

9. Eliot, *Selected Essays*, 352.

age. They are in a very real sense an expression of that spirit, albeit such an expression (certainly in the case of the more important art) no longer represents a common denominator.

It is, however, from a theological point of view of great importance that literature originating from a Christian culture still be taken seriously. To be sure, such products are unique artistic expressions and must in the first place be read and judged as such. They are unique creations, but they live and move in a universe of worth, one that bears the definite stamp of Christianity. In literature which emanates from a Christian era, this universe plays an often unconscious role in the free play of the imagination. In this manner the intuitions present implicitly can lead to new incarnations. These ideas and notions do not lie there ready at hand only to be decorated by the author. Therefore these intuitions are not only repetitions of well-known truths, but they can also lead to creative interpretations of a Christian vision of life. That is the reason why anyone interested in this legacy of Christian inspiration will be rewarded by taking it seriously. These are spirit-inspired works, and for those for whom it is possible to tend to such matters, the Holy Spirit is operative. These enrich theology through the sensibility of the authors who have received influences derived from concealed sources. Literary works participate in a very definite way in the mystery of the Christian gospel. They have a significance that must be sought, among other things, in expressing a Christological world, one that, in a certain sense, is the starting point of theology.

Compared with literature, theology can thus be seen as a down-to-earth affair. It needs the inspiration of literature to fend off superficiality, or boredom, or narrow-mindedness (to which theology is also prone). Literary writers also have a greater sensitivity and, therefore, have a greater insight into deeper levels of reality than theologians. Their object is life in general, and this freedom gives them their individual perceptions of reality. In the words of Balthasar: "In the great Catholic literary figures we find more originality and vibrance of thought—an intellectual life thriving superbly in a free and open landscape—than we do in the somewhat panting, long-winded theology of our time, which is satisfied with quite slender fare."[10]

---

10. Cited by Ed Block Jr., "Balthasar's Literary Criticism," in Oakes and Moss, eds., *The Cambridge Companion to Hans Urs von Balthasar*, 217.

The Post-Christian Era

With the above observations concerning literature of the Christian era, I do not intend to say that interest in literature must be limited to that literature alone. There is also non-Christian literature from the pre-Christian era that can serve a great purpose for the theologian. The great Greek writers (Homer, the tragedians, and the Romans (Vergil) are the first names that come to mind. But literature of the post-Christian era is likewise intriguing and relevant. In this post-Christian era we find authors and poets who often have undertaken solitary efforts as trailblazers to find out the way toward Christian belief experience and the adumbrations of that belief. In an era that seems "unpropitious" (T. S. Eliot), religious poetic art and literature are not easy to produce. Conversely, an era can be "too religious" for certain forms of Christian art, especially for literature and poetic art. So it happened in the Middle Ages when, despite an abundance of creative artists, not much great religious poetry came to be. On the other hand, the tension within one's own time can also generate work of a high order. These poets frequently draw from hidden wells that make great artistic achievements possible, works that clearly reveal a Christian inspiration. One thinks, for example, of G. M. Hopkins (England, nineteenth century) and T. S. Eliot (twentieth century). When it comes to writers of the romantic era, the names of the great Russians Tolstoy and Dostoevsky and the Scandinavian Selma Lagerlof come to mind. And why not cite Tolkien (*Lord of the Rings*) as well? Balthasar, in the citation above, aims at the French writers, Peguy, Claudel, and Bernanos. In The Netherlands some of the great twentieth-century writers were Christians, such as Gerrit Achterberg, Martinus Nijhoff, and Ida. M. Gerhardt. The scenario of a massive literary world closed off to religious writers is false and does great injustice to the reality of the situation. The scope of literature provides a wonderful space, and the great literature from one's own time finds an approach towards reality that, even if it is not intended to be the specific goal, testifies to a Christian inspiration. Thus it is that even where the theologian can easily sit in the prison of the taboos of his own time, it can happen that the author has the courage and inner freedom to spring this prison open.

It needs mentioning that important writers who view "gods and men" and "works and days" are not limited by their conscious reasoning. "Inspiration" is always more or less mechanical; that is to say, she presents forms of which the understanding of the inspired self will be unaware."[11] Here, in this context, configurations can arise which the writer himself has not conjured up but which have been urged upon him. Obviously, one detects here a role of the Holy Spirit, which one can never palpably demonstrate. The Christianized world has hidden layers that in unexpected moments can emerge from the dead and can gain a new life even long after the soul of the "once Christianized era" has departed.

Religious and Secular Art

There is such a thing as specifically religious art, especially in the "Christian era." There is, besides, a secular art. By making this distinction we mean something other than art in the "Christian" period and art in the "secular" period. Religious art is art which sustains an intentional relationship to religion, which means for us in the Western world primarily the Christian religion. There is a religious literary art in which the author in one way or another relates to a religious rendering of life and experience. According to T. S. Eliot, these poets are mostly minor poets, since they stake out a specific segment of human experience—the religious— and not the whole gamut of experience.[12] Obviously, there are exceptions, where the expression of the religious achieves an intensity and depth that in terms of human experience can stand in a relationship of the part to the whole of human experience. Milton is such an example. That is not intended to say anything negative about the work of minor poets, some of whom have also composed art of a high order. It hardly needs to be said that in different times religious art has devised different forms and content. In the Christian era this art is more objective, in the post-Christian era more subjective. In the first case we speak about a Christian commitment on the part of the writer. If he portrays the message of the gospel in his own words and images and gives his response to it, then he is asking the reader not to consider the expressed truths as his own discoveries. Rather, he is asking that these truths be compared to the standards that the literary work itself does not mention but assumes.

Where a reader and writer do not share a common Christian background, religious art must furnish (far more than otherwise) its own

11. Noordmans, "Iets over Dickens," 463.
12. Eliot, "Religion and Literature," in *Selected Essays*, 354.

references. This resembles the romantic view that a poem or literary work no longer has "merely" a referential function but creates its own meaning. A poem must, in both form and content, be original and should exhibit a unique thought and sensibility Each work must possess a form which authentically expresses the emotions. It is not an example of just anything but is a unique expression in which something is said that has not been said before. This approach leads ultimately to the "expressionism" of modern art.[13] The poet is seen as seer and prophet. Even though this religious-based art must be seen as authentic religious art, sometimes this form is incorrectly seen as the only possible form of such art. And that is one of the causes of the suspect glorification of the poet as seer and prophet, particularly if such a poet becomes a role model as an interpreter of the Christian message whether he is in or out of Schleirmacher's constellation—the theologian who calls these folks "religious virtuoses."[14]

There is also secular art. What comes into play here is the whole of human life and circumstances. This secular art can well be soundly religious in the broader sense of the word "religion." That does not show up explicitly, but far more implicitly. The writer thinks and writes out of a Christian thought and life-horizon. He creates work that could have proceeded only from a Christian imagination. This Christian thought and life-horizon constitutes a framework, a spiritual space, where within which this fictional world is set: the conditions that make the work possible and that, at the same time, provides an orientation. It is to be expected that such an implicitly Christian work of art would arise in a more or less Christianized culture but—since one age is not closed off from another, and since God's Spirit often chooses his own underground paths—such a work can also arise in other places.

Shakespeare is an example of secular art. He is not occupying a church office with official functions, and he does not image forth in his art any explicit religious experiences as a specific domain of human life. Still, his art is at the same time decidedly religious in the broader definition of that term. This study intends to show how this can be.

---

13. For this, see, among others, Taylor, *Sources of the Self*, 368–90, 456–94.

14. H. E. Mertens inclines to this view. See his "Schoonheid is uw naam," 174ff.

The Significance of Literature for Theology

After the above historical oversight, it is important to point out the relevance of literature for theology. Theology points directly to God's revelation. It regards this revelation as a perspective that lifts the curtain on authentic reality, especially since because the disclosure of reality gets articulated through judgment and ordeal. In that sense theology also emphatically speaks directly to the totality of human (and cosmic) reality. It can even be defended that reality shines forth only when it is seen in the light of God's revelation. Theology, however, does not have a monopoly on wisdom. It wrestles with reason and language to reflect on God's revelation as a revelation that gives true insight into reality—the more so since reality is not static but changes constantly. For that reason theology has ever since its infancy been interested in literature. Literature is a form of art. We can define literature with Lodewick as the creation of a new intensification of reality that satisfies and compels us and possesses enduring truth and that in literature is reached through language. This "creation" is in my opinion an "enduring truth" when it is based upon a "discovery" of reality.

The significance of literature in this sense can hardly be overestimated. A book "puts the axe in the frozen lake" of our every day experience of reality (Kafka). It opens a way to the unknown reality that lies hidden in the all-too-familiar, blunted or even contorted reality of our experience.[15] And since this way must be found and rediscovered by every generation, this remains an ongoing concern. Particularly, when we talk about "world literature," we do so as a manner of speaking. These discoveries have been made in such a blessed manner that here we can truly speak of lasting value. World literature is that literature that has discovered and given form to such an intensive unlocking of reality that it can always enable new generations of readers to gratify and be moved and stirred by it. In this literature one finds, through language, dimensions of reality which are "revelations." The theologian who reflects on the revelation of God and thereby delineates reality is by that act also heir of the unique human activity that conjures these dimensions and brings them up. It gives a heightened sense of reality—even heightened experience—because literature conveys experience with life.

---

15. Lodewick, *Literaire Kunst*, 8.

Language is the privileged medium for literature. Language is more than an external medium, as is the case, for example, in the sciences. We learn that literature is the ultimate involvement with language, not as a good in itself (this is not about language games), but as pointers to understand and disclose reality. Theology also concerns itself with language and seeks forms of expression that are advantageous to "belief which is thinking." This is a risky adventure, because this language is not simply there. In a sense this language must come to us as a gift of grace, and yet we have to engage in a process, a prolonged struggle for words and concepts. Theology demands not only a strict focus on its object, namely, God and his revelation, and not alone in disciplined thought and good reasoning in order to satisfy the adage "belief seeks insight" (*fides quaeri intellectum*), but it needs language as a medium. It is for that reason that the theologian is interested in literature and crosses the boundary that divides literature from theology. Insofar as theology is also a communication of the revelation of God, he searches for words so that the reality that inheres in revelation will shine forth. This is not a matter of picking up some words from literature, but being an interested party who carefully observes and listens to how literature explores language in its many forms so that aspects of reality can be disclosed and clarified. Out of the theologians's own mandate and naturally with his own vocabulary (think of the Bible and the language of tradition, also the theological tradition), he follows the poet. These words apply to him: "Since our concern was speech, and speech impelled us / To purify the dialect to the tribe / And urge the mind to aftersight and foresight."[16] The poet, "trying to learn to use words, in his fight to recover what has been lost/and found and lost again and again" is in that respect a companion of the theologian.[17] He provides enrichment. Therefore traffic needs to flow briskly beyond the theological border.[18]

Frontier Guards

After the previous discussion where I set forth the significance of literature for the theologian, it is of great importance first of all to state most emphatically that our border crossings can bear fruit only if theology and

16. Eliot, "Little Gidding," in *Four Quartets*.
17. Eliot, "East Coker," in *Four Quartets*.
18. See further, Laangenhorst, *Theologie & Literatur: Ein Handbuch*, 70, 231–4.

literature each preserve their own identity. The danger is real that we who come from theology create an artificial relationship with literature, one that virtually dissolves what is proper to theology. In view of the present situation it may be necessary to erect a danger sign. It is, for example, badly exaggerated, to see the relationship between the two as an incarnation "in which is met the human [literary] and the divine [the religious] in a united yet distinct partnership."[19] Using the incarnation as a model in this way imposes far too heavy a mortgage on the relationship, and is, more than that, a profanation of the incarnation.

Neither is it helpful for theology to wax lyrical about "a poetics of faith" or to posit a relationship between theology and literature through the concept of language and imagination. Indeed, language is a common concern of theology and literature. It is also true that there is a theology that makes use of poetry, drama, and narrative. Still, it is a bad prejudice to regard these theological forms as privileged ones, by which inevitably a lamentation arises over theology as being "too cut and dried," which is "reducing the essential mystery of ultimate reality to a set of clearly defined concepts."[20] To be sure, theology can be as dry as hay, but that is not because it is systematic. That would be as much as to say that vagueness is a better condition to trace the mystery of ultimate reality than doctrinal precision. This lamentation coincides with many others. Mertens joins the choir of lamenters when he speaks about "the scholastic juggling with such terms as substance, accident, essence, nature, person, and relations," and argues for "feeling, fantasy, expression."[21] When, next, he appeals to the Bible and to Jesus and insists that metaphorical pleading should be preferred, seeing that God is by definition unknowable, invisible, an entity not capable of comprehension, then we have, in my opinion turned to the wrong track.[22] Theology must not be ashamed of being theology. A healthy interaction with literature will be very productive and will surely prove helpful for interpreting the truth of the gospel, but these gains must not be used as a weapon leveled against theology or even against systematic theology itself. It is important that the theologian is more than "a dry systematizer." It is true that inspired writers appear on theological turf and that these very writers have been and always will be

---

19. David, *The Study of Literature and Religion: An Introduction*, 8.

20. Wright, *Theology and Literature*, 7.

21. Mertens, "Schonheid is uw naam," 75.

22. Ibid., 76.

a source of inspiration. There is a "bull market" in theological literature, and most certainly in practical theological discourse, that could be regarded as literature. However, these writers themselves frequently make use of systematic theology, and therefore it is unjust for them to seek as an alternative a more systematic theology. We ought to guard against a simplistic criticism of the systematic character of theology.

Here is another matter. Theology is a science, by which belief seeks insight. It seeks to understand the truth of revelation. Theology has as its presuppositions the revelation of God. It is a revelation whose basis and culmination are found in Jesus Christ, the Incarnate Word of God. Theology and diverse forms of religious discourse emanate from faith They are not closed off in some secure bastion of ecclesiastical complacency but relate in every possible way to the world beyond the church. Still, none of this can be understood without the idea of a revelation from God and a faith community that is consciously involved in relating to this revelation. Theology that takes another starting point, that distances itself from the idea of a special revelation, and that cuts itself from the faith community cannot, in a strict sense, be called theology, but should be looked on as philosophy or, more specifically, as philosophy of religion. Theology, then, is a science that requires commitment. It is not a free, uncharted searching expedition after truth but seeks the truth of the faith. The revelation of God is source and criterion of theology. That cannot be said about literature. That has its own truth domain. That is how it should be. It all goes unfortunately wrong, however, whenever the interaction of theology with literature proceeds in such a way that, in the process, theology forgets its own identity. Whenever theology and religion as a form of imagination is seen on a par with other forms of imagination that are seen as merely human products, then theology becomes a mere poetic of belief. The frontier between literature and theology then becomes raised because the boundary itself has been erased. Better still: theology has sold its own soul.[23]

The Critical Function of Theology

Theology is not literature, and literature is not theology. But literature does have a positive import for theology. Is the reverse also true? Does theology have an importance for literature? I believe that that is the case.

23. A recent example of this is H. Kuitert, *Hetzelfde anders zien, het christelijk geloof als verbeelding*.

Theology does not have only a questioning function, but also a critical one, a judging function. As I said earlier, seen from the point of view of modern literature, that will appear as a strange thought. The domain of literature is seen as autonomous. The only acceptable form of criticism is internal criticism—that is to say, criticism on the basis of literary criteria. Literature is not, however, value free. Every writer brings, consciously or unconsciously, a system of values with him and expresses those during the course of his work. All literature has influence, whether the quality be great or slight. It is, naturally, not possible to make out initially which system of values a writer employs—consciously or unconsciously—but the majority of writers swim with the stream of the spirit of the age and will surely bring that to expression in their work. T. S. Eliot, who as pioneer of the modern, twentieth-century writers, who can hardly be considered narrow-minded, states straightforwardly that the modern reader exposes himself to the mass movement of writers, each of whom claims to have written with an individual voice but who in reality are all moving in the same direction. He adds this: "There never has been a time, I believe, when the reading public was so large, or so helplessly exposed to the influences of its own time."[24] In a time when no theological background has formed a mutual code for the appraisal of literature, the morality in increasing measure becomes vulnerable to change through literature.

It is for that reason that a value system is necessary. As Eliot puts it: "Literary criticism should be completed by criticism from a definite and theological standpoint." And, "The greatness of literature cannot be determined solely by literary standards."[25] Theology has as its task to serve as an ethical critic, one which obviously does not leap to judgment, or exercise some authorized role, or assign itself the task of censorship, but gives a measured judgment. If it is good, then the theologically-based system of standards and criteria for the evaluation of literature that are based on these values are no obstacle to an encounter with literature but make possible a mutually enriching and analytical interaction. We expect contemporary writers to give voice to the spirits of their times, and it is hypocritical for them to stand ready to make all sorts of accusations against their age. Earlier I proposed what gain the theologian can derive from literature, and that applies also for modern literature. It is exactly the solidarity of the theologian with contemporary writers as they wrestle

24. Eliot, *Selected Essays*, 398.
25. Ibid.

together in order to reveal a new reality and to test new experiences which makes this relationship so important. However, this can be accomplished only through a system of values. This value system is essential, for without it the reader is on his own and is quickly delivered up to the literature. Without such a system one cannot develop his powers of discrimination, and that is regrettable. Literature must be grappled with, and besides the pleasure of the reading, there is also its inauguration into life. Literature can be of help in this way, but without proper criteria it can become a hazardous experience.

These critical observations point to another issue. Naturally, it is useful and necessary for one to read about his own times and with an open mind and respectful interest. But because this literature is immersed in the spirit of the time, it can do no harm to read literature from another era, and from places other than the Western world. Such readings in any case help us to rise above the limitations of the modern more productively. To cite Eliot once again: "We shall certainly continue to read the best of its kind, of what the time provides; but we must tirelessly criticize it according to our own principles, and not merely according to the principles admitted by the writers and by the critics who discuss it in the public press."[26]

And here is why I have specifically occupied myself with Shakespeare. Great literature of the past is not only literature whose worth has been proven and is, therefore, superior to most of contemporary literature. It is also literature out of another world with another value system, a system that is frequently inspired by a Christian spirit. It is sensible, therefore, to give it a place. It won't diminish your own spiritual world. Unfortunately, the life of the world shows little acquaintance with great literature of the past and gives it slight notice. At present, in high schools, that territory in literature is becoming in increasing measure a *terra incognita*. The helplessness of the reader can only grow greater through this neglect. It will require a special effort and resolve to reclaim this unknown territory in order to prevent its becoming an Atlantis—a reality about which we have heard only rumors.

26. Ibid., 401.

Bibliography

Ackroyd, Peter. *Shakespeare, de Biograffe.*

Aristotle. *Poetics* in *The Pocket Aristotle.* Translated by W. D. Ross. New York: Washington Square, 1958.

Auerbach, Eric. "Figura." *Archivum Romanicum* 22 (1938) 436–89.

———. *Mimesis.* Bern/Munchen, 1946.

Augustine. *De Genesis litteram libri duodecim.*

Bacon, Francis. *A Selection of His Works.* Toronto, 1945.

Balthasar, H. U. *Theodramatic I.* 1973.

Barth, Karl. *Kirchliche Dogmatic*, II, 2, 612-701.

Battenhouse, Roy. *Shakespeare's Christian Dimension: An Anthology of Commentary.* Bloomington: Indiana University Press, 1994.

Bernard of Clairvaux. "Hij kusse mij met de kus van zijn mond." In *Sermons 1–9.* Kampen, 1999.

Bethell, S. L. *Shakespeare and the Popular Dramatic Tradition.* New York: 1944/1997.

Birrell, T. A. *Engelse Letterkunde.* N.p.: Het Spectrum B.V., 1961.

Blake, William. "Auguries of Innocence." In *The Complete Works of William Blake*, edited by Geoffrey Keynes. 1966.

Bohren, Rudolf. *Geist und Gericht.* Neukirchen, 1979.

———. *Dass Gott schon wered.* Munchen, 1957.

Camus, Albert. *Le Mythe de Sisyphe.* Paris, 1942.

Collinson, Patrick. *The Religion of the Protestants.* Oxford, 1982.

Coppleston, F. *A History of Philosophy.* New York, 1962.

Curry, W. C. *Shakespeare's Philosophical Patterns.* Baton Rouge, 1937.

Danby, John. *Shakespeare's Doctrine of Nature.* London: Faber and Faber, 1949.

David, Jasper. *The Study of Literature and Religion: An Introduction.* London, 1989.

Eliot, T. S. *Four Quartets.* London: Faber and Faber, 1952.

———. *Selected Essays.* London, 1951.

Foakes, R. A., ed. *King Lear.* Arden Shakespeare Third Series. London: Thompson Learning, 2004.

Fokkelman, Jan, and Wim Wren, eds. *De Bibjel Literair.* Zoetermeer, 2003.

Freeman, John. "This Side of Purgatory: Ghostly Fathers and the Recusant Legacy in Hamlet," in *Shakespeare and the Culture of Christianity in Modern England*, 222–59. New York, 2003.

Frye, Northrop. *The Great Code: The Bible and Literature.* New York, 1991.

Frye, Roland M. *Shakespeare and Christian Doctrine.* 1963.

Garrick, David. *Testimonies to the Genius and Merits of Shakespeare.* 1769.

Geach, P. T. *The Virtues.* Cambridge, 1977.

Goppelt, L000. *Typos.* Darmstadt, 1973.

Greenblatt, S. "Shakespeare and the Exorcists." In *Shakespeare and the Question of Theory*.

Gunning, J. H. *Dante Alighieri, eene studie*. Amsterdam, 1879.

Halio, Jay L., ed. *King Lear*. The New Cambridge Shakespeare. New York: Cambridge University Press, 1992.

Hamilton, Donna B. "Shakespeare and Religion." In *The Shakespearean International Yearbook: Where Are We Now in Shakepsearean Studies?*, edited by Graham Bradshaw et al. Aldershot, UK: Ashgate 1999.

Hamilton, Donna B., and Richard Strier, eds. *Religion, Literature, and Politics in Post-Reformation England, 1540–1688*. Cambridge, 1996.

Heine, Heinrich. *Deutschland: Ein Wintermarchen*. Hamburg: Lampe, 1884.

Johnson, Samuel. *The Plays of Shakespeare*. Edited by D. F. Bratchell. London, 1990.

Jones, Norman. "Shakespeare's England," *A Companion to Shakespeare*, 39 ff.

Kastan, David Scott, ed. *A Companion to Shakespeare*. Oxford, 1999.

Kermode, Frank. *Shakespeare's Language*. New York, 2000.

———. "Our Muddy Vesture: Pacino's Merchant of Venice." *London Review of Books* 27/1 (January 6, 2005) 17.

Kierkegaard, Soren. *Het Begrip Angst*.

———. *Krankheit zum Tode*. Dunndruch-Ausgabe, Divbibliothek, Munchen, 1976.

Kish-Goodling. "Using *The Merchant of Venice* in Teaching Monetary Economics." *Journal of Economic Education* (Fall 1998).

Knight, G. Wilson. *The Crown of Life*. London, 1948.

———. *Shakespeare and Religion*. New York, 1968.

———. *The Wheel of Fire*. New York, 1949.

Kuitert, H. *Hetzelfde anders zien, het christelijk geloof als verbeelding*. Baarn, 2001.

Laangenhorst, Georg. *Theologie & Literatur: Ein Handbuch*.

Lamb, Charles. *The Works of Charles Lamb II*. 1818.

Lever, J. W., ed. *Measure for Measure*. In *The Arden Shakespeare Complete Works*. 2nd series. London: Methuen, 2004.

Lodewick, H. J. M. *Literaire Kunst*. Hertgenbosch, 1970.

McIlwraith, A. K., ed. *Five Elizabethan Tragedies*. London: Oxford University Press, 1971.

Melchior-Bonnet, Sabine. *The Mirror: A History*. Translated by Katherine H. Jewett. London, 2001.

Mertens, H. E. "Schonheid is uw naam," in *Essay over Esthetische and Religieuze ervaring*. Leuven, 1997.

Milward, Peter. *Shakespeare's Religious Background*. Bloomington: Indiana University Press, 1973.

Miskotte, K. H. *Messiaans verlangen and other literatuur—and cultuurkritische opstellen*. Kampen, 1999.

Nijenhuis. W. "Over heksen, demonen en demonologie: Shakespeare's *Macbeth* and the demonologie of Jacobus." *Kerk en Theologie* 42 (1991) 93–110.

Noble, Richmond. *Shakespeare's Biblical Knowledge*. 1935.

Noordmans, O. "Iets over Dickens." In *Verzamelde Werken*, V. Kampen, 1988.

———. "Mystiek in de moraal," in *Verzamelde Werken*, I. Kampen, 1978.

Oakes, Edward T., and David Moss. *The Cambridge Companion to Hans Urs von Balthasar*.

O'Donovan, Oliver. *Resurrection and Moral Order*. 2nd edition. Leicester, 1994.

O'Donovan, Oliver, and Joan Lockwood O'Donovan, eds. *From Irenaeus to Grotius: A Sourcebook in Christian Political Thought*. Translated by Mary Beas and Benjamin W. Farley. Grand Rapids, 1999.

Pascal, Blaise. *Pensees.* Various editions.

Richmond, Velma Bourgeois. *Shakespeare, Catholicism, and Romance.* New York, 2000.

Schneider, Th. "Shakespeare and Machiavelli." *Archiv fur Kulturgeschiche* 2. 1950.

Shaheen, Naseeb. *Biblical References in Shakespeare's Comedies.* Cranbury, NJ: Associated University Presses, 1993.

——. *Biblical References in Shakespeare's History Plays.* Cranbury, NJ: Associated University Presses, 1989.

——. *Biblical References in Shakespeare's Plays.* Lanham, MD: Rowan and Littlefield, 1999.

——. *Biblical References in Shakespeare's Tragedies.* Cranbury, NJ: Associated University Presses, 1987.

Shapiro, J. *Shakespeare and the Jews.* New York, 1996.

Shuger, Debora Kuller. *Habits of Thought in English Renaissance.* Berkeley, 1990.

Spencer, T. *Shakespeare and the Nature of Man.* 2nd edition. New York, 1958.

Spurgeon, C. *Shakespeare's Imagery and What It Tells Us.* Boston: 1958.

Taylor, Charles. *Sources of the Self: The Making of the Modern Identity.* Cambridge, 1989.

Taylor, Dennis, and David Beauregard. *Shakespeare and the Culture of Christianity in Modern England.* New York, 2003.

Tillyard, E. M. W. *Shakespeare's History Plays.* London, 1944.

——. *Shakespeare's Problem Plays.* 1951.

Van Dijk, Is. *Gezamenlijke geschriften* I/III. Groningen, 1917.

Van Gennep, F. O. *De Terugkeer van de verloren vader.* Baarn, 1989.

Van Haarneet. *A Declaration of Egregious Popish Impostures.* 1603.

Veldhuis, H. *Een Verzegeld boek: het natuurbegrip in de theologie van J. G. Manann (1730–1788).* Sliedricht, 1990.

Watson, Robert N. "*Othello* as Protestant Propaganda" in *Religion and Culture in Renaissance England,* edited by Claire Mceachern and Debora Shuger, 234–57. Cambridge, 1997.

Woldring, H. E. S. *Westerse waarden door Shakespeare Belicht.* Nijmegen, 2002.

Wright, T. R. *Theology and Literature.* Oxford, 1988.

Yeats, William Butler. *Essays.* New York, 1924.